Computing for the Terrified!

A simple introduction to personal computers
for anyone who is faced with using them for
the very first time

Steve Greenwood

Published by:

Computer Step
Unit 5c, Southfield Road
Southam, Leamington Spa
Warwickshire CV33 OJH
England

Tel. +44 (0)926 817999
Fax. +44 (0)926 817005

Printed in England

ISBN 1 874029 09 1

For my wife
Carol

About the Author

Steve Greenwood graduated in 1973 with an Honours Degree and is a chartered Engineer. Over the past twenty years, he has gained wide and varied experience in the design and application of computer systems, as business tools, product development tools and as integral parts of larger systems.

The author of the popular book "Computers in Schools" - also published by Computer Step - Steve has presented many successful courses on the subject of personal computers.

Preface

There are many books available covering the basics of personal computers, so why on earth did I write yet another?

Quite simply, I have found that many people are so frightened of the whole subject that they dare not even start reading any such book for fear of appearing stupid.

At the same time, many people - whilst not even remotely interested in any form of computing - have suddenly found that these infernal machines are now a fact of life in many companies and anyone changing jobs or returning to work after a prolonged absence - perhaps to raise a family or because of redundancy - can find that a basic knowledge of personal computers is helpful - or even essential - in coming to terms with this modern working environment.

The title of the book was chosen with this in mind!

The book has been based on my personal experience gained both from working with computers and - more recently - with presenting training courses to people who - just like yourself - have realised that they simply must come to terms with this "terrifying" subject.

I hope you will enjoy reading this book and that you will then feel much more confident to use computers in the future.

Contents

Chapter 1. Introduction

A SHORT TIME ago, I was asked to present a training course at a well-known College of Further Education. The conversation went something like this:

"We are getting lots of requests - from people who would like to change jobs or who want to return to work after a number of years away - who are finding computers in use virtually everywhere. They are terrified of them! Can you put together a short course to overcome this fear and break through the jargon barrier?"

Following a lot of hasty work, I compiled such a course and presented it to groups of frightened students. In all cases and after only a few hours, the fear began to disappear and computers became less of a mystery. I was so impressed with the success of these courses that I decided to make the information more widely available.

I realise that not everyone has the time (or money) to attend such a course and so the idea emerged of producing this simple but effective book. It covers the subject of the very basics of Personal Computers - as used in many business offices. It has been designed for anyone who has no previous knowledge of computers and who wants to feel more confident about using them in the future.

The book is organised in short chapters, each covering a particular topic. These topics are presented in simple English, steering away from computer jargon whenever possible. On few occasions when jargon has been used, it is described in detail, again using simple English. You should also refer to the glossary at the end for explanations on commonly-used computer terms.

Objectives of this book

This book *is not* designed to teach you how to operate a word processor or a spreadsheet. You can do these things and more on a personal computer and there are other useful books published by Computer Step, on these subjects - see the list at the back. The book *is* designed to make you feel more comfortable with using such a machine for any application you may encounter in the workplace. It also provides an insight into the many and varied uses such a machine can be put, together with an overview of some of the jargon which is so frequently used.

At the moment, the computer may be a mystery to you - you may even be frightened of touching it. After reading this book and completing some of the exercises, you will probably not be an expert, but I trust that you will at least be less intimidated by the thought of having to use one.

We start off by looking at what a computer is and in particular, what an IBM PC-compatible computer is. In a simple short chapter we will take the first step of switching on the PC. We then take a look at the actual hardware - the physical bits and pieces before moving on the big subject of software. What exactly is software? What is a file? an operating system? an application program? Once we have an understanding of these basic principles we start to move on to the more practical side. What can we use a PC for? What might go wrong? Finally we take a look at the direction the personal computer market is heading in and suggest some "next steps" when you feel confident to take them.

It will be a great help if you have a PC-compatible computer to use as you go through the book (we will explain the term "PC-compatible" shortly). If you don't, you should still learn a lot about computers in general and PCs in particular, simply by reading through the book.

We cover a lot of ground, and it is more important for you to effectively cover a small amount at a time, rather than racing through the entire book, leaving yourself bewildered and baffled. Please take your time and progress at your own speed. In that way, you will gain most benefit from reading this book.

An explanation of the conventions used

As I have already mentioned, we will steer away from computer jargon wherever possible. There are however a few conventions used in the book. These are explained here.

Text printed like that shown indicates that the text would be displayed on the computer display:

> **This is text as displayed by the computer**

> <cr> will be used to indicate pressing a key (on the keyboard) called "Enter" or "Carriage Return".

> <esc> will be used to indicate pressing another special key called the "Escape" key.

These and other special keys are covered later.

PC

> will be used to refer to IBM compatible personal computers in general. These may be IBM PCs, PC or PC-AT compatibles, IBM PS/2s or other similar machines.
>
> Again, these terms are covered later.

Disk

> is the computer term for a type of digital storage medium.

Program

> is the computer term for a set of instructions given to a computer to perform a specific task.

Operating System

> is a set of programs that allow you to control, manage and use your computer and it's components.

DOS

> is the IBM registered name used for the original standard PC operating system (PC-DOS). For the purposes of this book, DOS is also used interchangeably with MS-DOS, the Microsoft name for (essentially) the same operating system. For completeness, a company called Digital Research have an operating system called DR-DOS which is also compatible with DOS! (This is particularly popular on battery-operated PCs, due to its power-conservation features).

A more comprehensive glossary of terms is provided at the end of the book.

In order for a Personal Computer (PC) to be of any use for serious work, it must have a reliable means of storing programs and data. Most PCs use rotating magnetic discs (usually spelled the American way - disks). Disks can be removable (floppy disks) or fixed to the machine (hard disks). Hard disks are more expensive than floppy disks and can contain much more data.

PCs were originally manufactured with floppy disk drives
(usually two of them) and no fixed (hard) disk drives. This
meant that all programs, data and even the operating system
(DOS) was stored on floppy disks and had to be loaded by hand
each time the machine was started. As with all other hardware,
hard disk drives are much less expensive than they were ten
years ago and most of these machines that are still used for
business purposes have now been "up-graded" by the fitting of
a hard disk. For the purpose of the book, we will assume that
the machine you will use is fitted with a hard disk, although
much of the information will still apply to a floppy-disk
machine.

Chapter 2. What is a Computer?

IN ORDER TO understand what a computer is, we need to spend a few minutes looking "under the skin". I promise I will not spend much time discussing the intimate technical details of the computer's inner workings but we do need to spend a short time looking at a few basic principles. This will then make it far easier to understand the uses - and limitations - of PCs.

So, let us now have a look at both a little bit of theory and a little history, from which we will then see how these factors have shaped the familiar computers as found now in most offices.

What can a Computer do?

What exactly is a computer, you may ask? A computer is simply a machine that processes information (the *input*) in a way defined by a series of instructions (the *program*) and then produces some form of result (the *output*).

For example, a computer may be used for forecasting the weather. Such a machine would be supplied with a stream of data (the *input*) from sensors monitoring wind, atmospheric pressure, etc. and then would produce a weather forecast (the *output*) as a result of analysing this data (as defined by the *program*). This particular example is also a good illustration of another very important fact with computers. The quality of the output is only as good as the original data; rubbish in, rubbish out!

Putting this more generally, a computer can perform tasks as defined by the application software if these tasks are within the limitations of the machine itself. This includes any external devices[1] (such as printers) that may be connected to it. The more powerful the computer is, the quicker it can perform a particular task but, to state the obvious, a powerful computer running the best word processor software in the world cannot produce the simplest letter if it does not have a printer attached.

In other words - the computer hardware, its software and its peripherals must all be matched to the task in hand - and by running the appropriate software, the same computer can be made to perform totally different tasks.

Examples of typical computer programs that are in widespread use are:

- Wordprocessor
- Spreadsheet
- Database
- Accounting

We will look in detail at these different types of uses or *applications* later in the book.

What is an IBM PC-compatible Computer?

Now we have begun to understand what a computer is, what on earth is an IBM PC?

---

[1] *External items of hardware (such as printers) are known as peripherals. We will discuss the many different types of peripherals that are available later in the book.*

Back in the early 1980s, IBM invented a small personal computer- the PC. It was not considered very important by IBM (or anyone else) at that stage. Because of this, its design was not well protected - its design had an open architecture - and it was therefore easy to copy and expand.

IBM and others then began to realise the potential of the PC and it quickly became the world standard - largely because it was backed by IBM's name. Literally hundreds of IBM-compatible machines then flooded the market from new companies set up specifically to address this new market. These machines appeared at much lower prices and, ironically, IBM lost control of the market that their own name had established!

In order for a computer to be totally IBM PC-compatible it must comply with a number of different standards that were embodied in the original design:

- Software compatible - To be able to load software labelled "for the PC" and run it without problems.

- Hardware compatible - Expansion cards, display devices (monitors) and connections to peripherals must be identical.

- User compatible - Even the keyboard layout should be standard.

This has resulted in many different makes of machines, but many have a very familiar look about them, usually with three main parts - the main system unit, the keyboard and the visual display or monitor, all described in more detail in chapters 4-5.

A bit of Jargon

Before delving in deeper into the PC's workings, now is a good time to describe a few terms that will be frequently encountered when reading about or using PCs.

The Cursor	The cursor is simply an indicator, saying where any keyboard characters will be placed on the screen. It may look like an underscore (_) character or a solid block and usually flashes on and off.
Bits	The smallest unit of data.
No. of bits	A measure of the CPU (Central Processing Unit) power.
Byte(s)	A memory "slot" that can store 1 character.
Kilobyte (K)	A thousand bytes or 1024 exactly.
Megabyte (MB)	A million bytes or a thousand kilobytes.
MS-DOS	Microsoft PC-standard Disk Operating System.
Megahertz (MHz)	A measure of the speed or power of the processor.

For those of a more inquisitive nature, a fuller list of jargon is provided for reference in the glossary at the end of the book.

A Brief history of Personal Computing

There is some disagreement over who invented the computer. Charles Babbage is often quoted as the inventor of the first computer, back in the 1800s. However, his analytical engine was never built. The first computer to run a program stored in memory was built at Manchester University in the late 1940s. That was a large floor-standing monster that needed rather more than a desk to sit on top of, and it took nearly an hour to come up with the answer to a simple maths problem!

In this book, of course, we are talking about personal computers and again, it is difficult to be precise as to when they first appeared, since personal computers really evolved rather than being invented. Commodore designed the now distant "PET" computer, Apple invented the original Apple I computer, this was followed by ACT's Apricot...... and of course there was the Sinclair ZX80 from Clive Sinclair's (until then) audio products company. All these computers were incompatible with one another and needed software, expansion modules and even some peripherals that were dedicated totally to the particular unit. Most of these computers were designed for use as toys and, initially, they gave an unprofessional image to the "home computer" marketplace.

It wasn't until the IBM PC was introduced in 1981 that the PC standard was defined and now - with the backing of IBM - the era of personal computing really started.

It now seems almost unbelievable that the original IBM PC - launched in August 1981 - came with only 64K of memory (most new systems are supplied with at least 30 times this amount), no hard disk drive, monochrome monitor and audio-cassette interface (for bulk data storage!) and cost in excess of £2000.

IBM had delayed the machine's launch until the spreadsheet program "VisiCalc" was available for the new machine and, even so, sold over 10,000 machines in the rest of the year and over 150,000 in 1982. Once the potential of these machines was realised, their development really began to snowball, as can be seen below:

YEAR	MACHINE	DESCRIPTION
1981	IBM PC ACT Sirius	8088 8-bit processor.
1982	PC clones	IBM compatible machines from other manufacturers.
1983	IBM PC-AT	80286 16-bit - more computing power.
	Apple Lisa	Revolutionary Graphical User Interface (not PC compatible).
1984	PC-AT clones	Supplied by many new companies.
	Apple Macintosh	New generation using Graphical User Interface.
1986	IBM PS/2 range	Micro-Channel architecture. Still PC compatible (different expansion cards).
1988	PC-AT 'Super-clones'	80386 32-bit, massive increase in power.
1990	Faster clones	80486 processor, even more computing power.
1993+	Hyper-speed clones	P5 Pentium processor

It is now estimated that there are around 50 million PCs and compatibles world-wide.

Common types of Computers today:

Following the initial glut and variety of PCs, many of the original manufacturers have failed to survive the terrific competition that there has been in this mad market-place. As a result, there are now a number of relatively well established suppliers of PC products. Each has its own range of similar machines at similar prices. This can be seen by flicking through any of the vast number of computer magazines available at newsagents.

PC-compatibles:

- PC-AT 286 / 386 clones
- 80486 and Pentium (586)-powered machines
- IBM PS/2 range

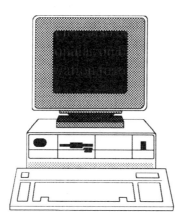

An IBM PS/2

Other non-compatible machines:

- • Apple Macintosh range
- • Commodore Amiga
- • Acorn Archimedes range

IBM no-longer support the PC standard directly. This is largely the result of them realising their mistake in not protecting the original PC design more thoroughly. Instead, IBM now supply models based on their PS/2 range. These are still PC software compatible, with most models featuring a new registered proprietary design for the internal "bus" (we will talk about buses later). This has all been done in an attempt to regain control of the personal computer market. IBM have recently introduced further models targeted at the lower end of the market. To date, this strategy has only been partly successful, with PC-clones still more popular than the IBM products in the market place.

Ironically, if IBM had protected the original PC design, there would have been less competition and no price war between manufactures and as a result, the PC would probably not have been as successful as it is today!

Chapter 3. Switching On

MANY PEOPLE ARE frightened of turning a PC on. Do not be!
The switch may be found on the back, side or front. Please note
that you may also find it necessary to separately switch on the
monitor (display). Some monitors are powered from a switched
mains outlet on the PC base unit, whilst others are powered
directly from a separate mains supply.

Whenever a PC is switched on, it will go through its own start-
up routine. It may appear as though the machine has a mind of
its own. It will begin to perform a number of actions
automatically as defined by a tiny computer program. This
program is stored permanently in a small memory chip called
the BIOS (Basic Input/Output System) - found on the
computer's main circuit board - the motherboard.

This program is the only "intelligence" available to the
computer at this stage. It is the BIOS which directs the PC to
first perform some routine tests to check the health of the
computer hardware. Having done this, it then instructs the PC
to search for and then load the operating system into the
computer's memory.

An operating system is simply a particular type of computer
program which allows the user to begin to communicate with
the computer. There are several of these operating systems that
can be used on a PC but on most, it will be MS-DOS. This will
be held as a number of special files on the computer's hard disk
and which will be loaded into memory at this time.

This process is known as "booting" - a strange expression describing how the computer "pulls itself up by its own boot-laces". When the operating system is loaded, the computer can then obey commands from and respond to the user - it becomes more intelligent.

The DOS prompt

DOS informs the user that it is ready to accept a command by displaying the DOS "prompt", which is normally displayed at the left-hand side of the monitor screen, as follows:

    A>

This prompt tells the user that the floppy disk (known as A:) is the "active" drive.

    C>

This prompt tells the user that the hard disk (known as C:) is the "active" drive.

Changing the DOS prompt

The exact form of the prompt message (or prompt string as it is often called) can be determined by the user using a DOS command called "PROMPT". For now, we will not worry too much about what a DOS command is, but by using this facility, the DOS prompt can easily be changed to something which can give us useful additional information. It is usual to use the following prompt on a hard-disk machine:

    C:\>

This prompt indicates the current drive (C:) and sub-directory, currently the root directory(\).

C:\APPS\WORDPROC>

This prompt indicates that C: is still the current drive and we are now in the **WORDPROC** sub-directory of the **APPS** directory.

We will learn all about directories and sub-directories shortly.

DOS will support up to two floppy disks and these are always known as A: and B: (if fitted).

There may be other hard disk drives fitted to the machine and these would have successive letters (D:, E:, etc) associated with them. These letters are allocated automatically by DOS.

Chapter 4. The Hardware

YOU WILL OFTEN hear the term "hardware" in connection with the subject of computers. This is simply the term used for the physical bits and pieces that make up the computer. This chapter describes the important items of hardware in a PC.

The main components of a PC

There are many different types of PCs now in use, from "Palm-Top" and "Notebook" portables through to large "Tower" systems. The vast majority, however, are designed to be used on the desk and consist of three main boxes.

The System unit

Usually a metal or plastic box and housing the majority of the workings of the computer, the System unit will contain:

- The motherboard - the heart of the unit
- The power supply
- Disk drives
- Expansion cards

The unit will have one or more openings in the front panel for the insertion of floppy disks and - possibly - CD ROM disks and tape cartridges.

Some models also have a "Reset" switch as an alternative method of re-booting[2] (re-starting) the computer, a "Turbo" switch to select a higher CPU speed and a number of LED indicator lights. Under normal conditions, these switches should not be touched.

System units vary in shape and size and most have the on-off switch mounted inconveniently on the side or rear panel.

The Keyboard

The keyboard provides the main means of entering data on most computers. Its layout represents a normal QWERTY (named after the first six alphabetic keys on the keyboard) typewriter keyboard, with extra keys around the periphery.

Function keys (F1, F2........, F12) are used by application programs for specific purposes. Such applications often provide a keyboard template to more easily identify the functionality of such keys.

Most keyboards also include a separate numeric pad and cursor control keys.

Some important keys

Many of these "extra" keys are used only occasionally, whilst others are in constant use with most applications. Here is a list of the more commonly used ones:

---

[2] *The term "booting" is explained in more detail in chapter 6.*

Enter Key

Press this key after typing a command from the keyboard. It is only then that your computer will try and interpret your command. Also used as a 'carriage return' on a typewriter to mark the end of a paragraph.

 Shift Key

Directly equivalent to the "shift" key on a typewriter, pressing <shift> enables upper case (capital) letters and alternate punctuation characters to be entered.

 Caps (Capital) Lock

Similar to "shift lock" on a typewriter keyboard, this key has a "toggle[3]" effect and its state is usually indicated by a small lamp (LED) on the keyboard. When <caps lock> is enabled (the LED is on), all letters are entered as upper case. Note that if <shift> is pressed at the same time, this has the effect of temporarily de-selecting <caps lock> and lower case characters are then selected. <caps lock> only affects alphabetic characters and not

---

[3] *A "toggle" is where an operation (i.e. pressing the key) causes an action to take place (enabling the "caps lock" function) and performing the same action (pressing the key again) reverses that action ("caps lock" is disabled).*

numeric or punctuation characters. This is different to
the "shift lock" key found on typewriters. Typists please
note that there is no "shift lock" key on a PC keyboard.

Escape Key

Often used to tell the computer that the next keystrokes
are going to be instructions, or to tell the computer to
"Exit" the application. This depends upon the particular
application software in use. For example, when at the
DOS prompt, <esc> simply cancels any preceding
characters that have been typed.

Delete Key

Used to delete the character to the right of the current
cursor position (dependent on the application program).

Backspace Key

Usually used to delete the character to the left of the
current cursor position (dependent on the application
program).

Home Key

Usually moves the cursor to the beginning of the current
line.

Page Up

Moves the cursor and displayed area by one screenful towards the beginning of the document.

 Page Down

Moves the cursor and displayed area by one screenful towards the end of the document.

 End Key

Usually moves the cursor to the end of the current line.

 Cursor Arrow Keys

These keys are used to move the cursor around the screen, one character at a time.

 Function Key 1

Often used to access the "on-line help" facility when running an application program. Again, very dependent upon the application software. This key has no effect when pressed at the DOS command prompt.

There are 11 other function keys (F2-F12) - they can all be programmed by applications for specific functions.

Control & Alt (Alternative) Keys

Used together with other keys (usually one at a time), these keys modify the meaning of any other key pressed at the same time.

     Tab Key

Moves the cursor (insertion point) to the next tab stop (like a typewriter). By pressing <shift> and <tab> together, a "back-tab" (reverse tab) character is obtained, moving the cursor to the left by one tab stop.

These keys are used very often, and there are also many other special keys, which generally are used only in specialist applications.

Note:

During the life of the PC, there have been a number of different keyboard layouts used. On "full size" keyboards, all have the above keys. Early PCs have 83 or 84 keys whilst nearly all PC-AT and later machines have "extended" keyboards with 102 keys (101 in the USA). In all cases they are based on the standard typewriter QWERTY keyboard layout (in this country). The number and position of the other keys is the only thing that changes. An exception to this rule is that on some miniature PCs such as palm-tops, you will find that some compromises have been made in order to minimise the size of the keyboard whilst still retaining the correct key spacing.

The Display

The third major item is the Display, or Monitor. Most displays use the same technology as a television to present information to the user. In the early days of computers, most displays were monochrome (black and white) but colour is now the norm.

Displays are available in different grades, as defined (largely) by their resolution. This is a measure of the number of separate points or "pixels" available on the screen. The higher the resolution, the better the quality of display, all other factors being equal.

Early machines were supplied with very low resolution monochrome (MDA) or colour (CGA) displays, totally unsuitable for most applications today. Soon, IBM started the trend to higher resolution monitors with the introduction in the mid 1980s of their EGA (Enhanced Graphics Adapter, 640 x 350 pixels), quickly followed by the VGA (Video Graphics Array, 640 x 480 pixels).

Today, VGA and Super-VGA (800 x 600 minimum) are the minimum resolution considered suitable for serious work.

In addition, there are many third-party suppliers of specialist (usually higher resolution) displays for such applications as advanced CAD (Computer-Aided Design).

Chapter 5. Hardware in more detail

HAVING NOW TAKEN a brief look at the main physical items in a PC, let us now look "under the skin" to explain a little about the major internal parts of the machine.

A Quick Look Inside

If we open up the case of a PC, we see a variety of circuit boards and other items which combine to form the computer itself. The main elements are shown in the block diagram below.

Block Diagram of a PC

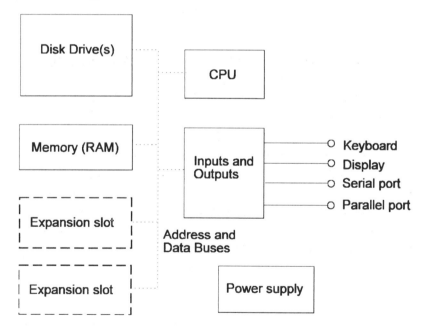

The Central Processor Unit - The CPU

The actual central processing "heart" of the PC is actually a microprocessor (usually abbreviated to mpu). This performs all the calculations and controls all the other hardware. There are many different microprocessors available in the electronics world, made by a number of different companies. When the original PC was designed, IBM chose a mpu manufactured by the Intel company - the 8088 - to "power" its new machine. As a result, to maintain compatibility, all PC compatibles use similar microprocessors and since that time, a range of more and more powerful compatible microprocessors has been developed.

The power of the processor is measured by both its size (number of bits) and its speed (MHz).

Processor type	Specification	Performance
8088	8 bit 4.77MHz	(very) slow
80286	16 bit 20MHz	slow
80386	32 bit 16MHz	medium
80486	32 bit 33MHz	fast
P5 or Pentium[4]	64 bit 66MHz	ultra fast

---

[4] *Intel were originally going to call this processor the 80586, but a recent court case resulted in a ruling that it was not possible to patent such a number. This caused Intel to change to this rather more esoteric name.*

There are of course many variants on the above examples and many other factors which affect the speed or power of a particular PC. Nevertheless, these two factors give a good initial guide to the machine's capabilities.

Memory (RAM)

RAM is an abbreviation for "Random Access Memory". This is the temporary storage area used by the CPU - where the live program and data files are stored. RAM does not retain its memory when power is removed from the computer.

The amount of memory that is installed is another factor which determines the power of a PC.

Most memory in a PC is a particular type of RAM called DRAM - Dynamic Random Access Memory. We will not delve into the electronics of this any deeper as things may start to get a little complicated. Suffice to say that as far as the user is concerned, there is no difference between RAM and DRAM.

DRAM memory devices (chips) have come down dramatically in price over the past five years. At the same time, modern computer software packages - particularly those for graphics and multi-media - demand more and more memory before they will operate efficiently. Early PCs were often fitted with only 256kB of memory. This was then considered to be enough memory for most requirements but as the industry developed, 640kB became the standard requirement for running most "serious" packages. This particularly strange figure is arrived at because DOS can only directly support this amount of memory. When the PC was designed, this limit seemed irrelevant as earlier computers could only support 64kB of memory, but with the development of more powerful applications, the limit became very restrictive.

Another limiting factor was that early machines using the 8088 processor could only directly address at total of 1MB of memory.

This limit was removed by the arrival of the 80286 processor (which could address 16MB), but in the interests of compatibility (and price!), this extra range was not utilised in the early days of these machines.

Even today, the 640kB RAM-size limit is still the case for DOS applications and different ways have been adopted for overcoming this limit, allowing modern PC applications to use up to the full 16MB of memory!

Memory Expansion

Since PCs were introduced, memory prices have been decimated and, at the same time, PCs have become used more and more as serious computing machines. As already mentioned, different techniques have been adopted for overcoming these memory limits and for the technically minded, this topic is discussed in more detail here. For the non-technical, it may be better to skip this section, or at least leave it until a second reading. I would hate to confuse you by delving too deeply at this stage!

Expanded Memory

Expanded memory was the initial technique used by hardware and software companies to overcome the "1MB" barrier of the 8088 mpu as used in the original PC. The best supported standard is the "LIM V4.0" (Lotus, Intel, Microsoft, version 4) standard, whereby it was possible to shoe-horn several extra MB of memory into the PC and to access it through a tiny 64kB "window". This technique is known as "paged memory" and is relatively slow, but is the only means of increasing the available memory on 8088-based machines.

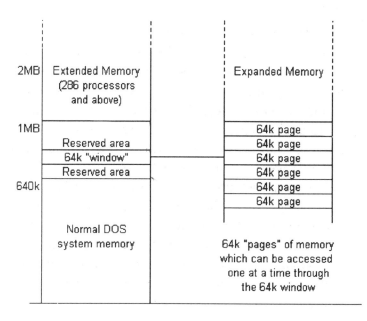

Extended Memory

Extended memory is now the standard technique of
increasing the memory size on modern PCs, overcoming
the 1MB limit of the early 8088-based machines. This
technique can only be used on 80286 (or higher)
processors. Extended memory simply uses the linear
addressing space above 1MB, and therefore give fast
access to this memory. It does this at the expense of
losing compatibility with 8088-based PCs. (In the
1990s, this is not much of a loss!) It does however mean
that this is one reason why certain applications will only
work on 80286 machines and above.

Ram-disk and Memory caches

Here are two further uses of RAM that increase system
efficiency. A RAM disk was often used in early PCs as a
means of gaining an extra disk space (at the expense of
losing some of the available memory). This involves
using a special program (or software driver, as it is
known) to allow some of the memory to simulate a disk
drive. This drive is then available as (say) drive D:,
although no such drive actually exists. Any data written
to the drive is lost when the machine is switched off.
The main benefit of such a drive is to speed up the
operation of disk-intensive programs. The RAM disk is
much faster than a hard or floppy disk drive. Certain
applications can benefit from this technique if correctly
configured.

With the advent of cheaper and larger memory, a more
usual way to speed-up disk access is to use a memory
cache. This is again achieved by using a different type of

software driver. The cache can be best thought of as a "buffer store" which stores frequently used parts of application files. Again, the memory has faster access time than the disk and this can result in the speeding up of application programs. A benefit over a RAM disk is that a cache program can automatically back up any changes to disk so that data is not lost when the computer is turned off.

Memory (ROM)

For completeness, ROM (read-only memory) is used for permanent storage of permanent small programs. In the PC, these are used to store the instructions needed by the microprocessor when power is first switched on and for other basic utility routines. The collective term used for such a collection of small programs is a BIOS - Basic Input Output System. The BIOS is the only part of the original PC's design to have been protected by IBM. It is this that defines precisely how the CPU communicates with the "outside world". Several specialist BIOS companies have now successfully reproduced the functionality of the BIOS without breaking the IBM copyright.

The real-time clock

All PCs have some means of keeping a record of the current time and date. Early machines needed to have these details entered every time the PC was switched on. Newer machines have a clock "chip" powered by the same battery as the CMOS

RAM[5]. This allows all software files to be "stamped" with the time and date of their creation or last modification - useful for back-up and file sorting purposes. The time and date is displayed alongside each filename when the DIR (directory) command is typed, as shown below:

`C:\PROJECTS\BOOKS>dir`

```
Volume in drive C is 11OCT91
Volume Serial Number is 1234-ABCD
Directory of C:\PROJECTS\BOOKS

.              <DIR>       29/11/92   16:18
..             <DIR>       29/11/92   16:18
SB0001    01      149310 04/08/93   21:40
SB0001    DOC     211379 12/10/93   11:05
SB0002    DOC       6600 05/09/93   17:11
SB0003    D1      217191 14/02/93   21:49
SB0003    D2      225065 07/03/93   21:53
SB0004    DOC       8246 05/12/92   17:06
         8 file(s)       817791 bytes
                        26828032 bytes free
```

`C:\PROJECTS\BOOKS>`

In the above example, the DOS "directory" command DIR has been typed at the DOS prompt. In this particular sub-directory, there are six files displayed, all with their time and date of creation. You may also notice that there are also two other

---

[5] *CMOS RAM is a type of memory used for permanent storage of certain "set-up" information. Please refer to the section on Set-up in chapter 11.*

mysterious files called ".". and "..". These are simply small internal files DOS uses to keep track of where the particular sub-directory "lives". We will look at DOS commands, files, backups and sub-directories later in the book.

Floppy Disks and Hard Disks

Disks are rotating magnetic storage devices, used for storing program files and data.

A floppy disk

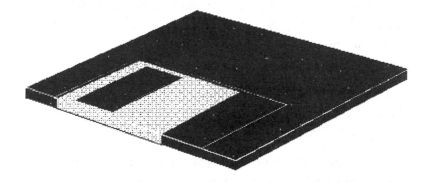

Floppy disks are removable from the machine and vary in storage capacity from 360K to 2.8MB. They are typically 5¼" (flexible) or 3½" (rigid case) in size.

You must NOT touch the exposed disk surface! Grease from fingers can attract dirt particles which can then cause data loss and even damage the head in the disk drive itself.

Similarly, you must only write on the label with a felt-tipped pen. A ball-pen can cause indentations which may deform the magnetic surface of the disk, again making it unreadable.

A PC may contain up to two floppy disk drives. These are known as drives A: (and B:, if fitted).

Hard disks

Hard disks are fixed non-removable devices and can vary in size from 10MB to greater than 1GB (1000MB). They have much faster access times (the time taken to read or write to a particular track or part of disk) than floppy disks. To the user, this means that any program running from them will run much faster. In the early days of PCs, hard disk drives were a luxury available only to the privileged few. Now, it is difficult to imagine using a PC which did not have at least a 20MB hard disk attached. Today, 80MB is about the smallest realistic size for serious business use.

The first hard disk on the PC is known as drive C:, even if no drive B: is fitted. A PC may contain more than one hard disk, in which case subsequent drives would be known as D:, E:, etc., although this is a little unusual.

As will be seen later, DOS has evolved in many steps from its original version 1.0 to the current release. During this evolution, DOS has been expanded to improve its power and functionality and also to keep up with hardware developments. Earlier versions of DOS had a fixed-disk "partition" size limit of 32MB. Multiple partitions then had to be used with large disks, so that DOS could treat them as several smaller disk drives. This resulted in a single disk having a C:, D:, E: etc., partition, depending on the size of the drive. This restriction was removed with the advent of DOS version 4.00.

Disk Formatting

Although both floppy and hard disks are mechanically very different, they are virtually identical as far as the computer is concerned (apart from their capacity, of course). There are therefore many similarities in the way data is stored and retrieved on both types of disks.

To use any disk, it must be "formatted" before it can be used. To do this, the DOS command

```
Format
```

is used. Formatting will destroy any data on the disk, so be careful.

If the MS-DOS system files are required on the disk, the disk should be formatted using a slight variation on this command, by typing

```
Format /S
```

The "/S" is known as a command line switch, which is a very grand way of saying that it slightly modifies the basic command. Many DOS commands will accept such switches and these are listed in the MS-DOS reference manual which should accompany your PC.

Other Disk-based Storage devices

For completeness, we will briefly cover the other rotating storage devices that you may encounter.

CD-ROM

Compact discs are now well established in the hi-fi arena. They provide high quality sound which is recorded in a digital format. They are therefore also suitable for permanent (read only) storage of other types of data and are now being used for storage of archive (permanent) data on PC and other computer systems. Each CD will store over 400MB of data, equivalent to over 50,000 pages of closely typed text! Typical applications include archived databases and picture libraries.

Some CD-ROMs now also support the new Kodak "Photo-CD" standard. These "multi-session" drives allow ordinary photographs to be incorporated into documents or multimedia PC training courses.

CD-Interactive

A special type of CD-ROM used for advanced interactive training and simulation/games applications. These programs can combine program, sound, graphics and video information.

WORM drives

Optical drives that can be written to (programmed) only once, and read multiple times (Write Once Read Many). These are far less common than CD-ROM drives.

Floptical Disks

Floptical disks combine the technologies of optical storage and floppy disks to provide a high-density and low cost removable storage medium.

Serial and Parallel Ports

These are the two main types of ports, used for connecting the computer to peripherals such as printers. If the printer has a serial port, it must be connected to a similar serial port on the computer.

The Parallel port

Parallel ports are unidirectional (output only) and usually communicate with other devices without any need to configure the machine(s). Usually, these are used for direct connection to printers. Parallel ports require a multi-wire interconnecting cable which must be restricted to five or six metres in length.

DOS supports up to two parallel ports.

The Serial port

Serial ports are bi-directional and are used for connection to peripherals such as modems, scanners, other computers and certain types of printers. Serial ports have the advantage of only requiring three wires in the interconnecting cable, which can be up to fifty metres or more in length. They do however require that many variables are set up correctly[6] that it can often seem like black magic is needed to establish reliable communications.

---

[6] *You may hear of baud rate, parity, DCE or DTE devices, number of stop bits, etc, to mention just a few possible parameters of a serial link which must be set correctly before a reliable communications channel is established.*

DOS originally provided for just two serial ports until version 3.3, which introduced support for four ports.

The In-Port

Recently, a new standard, the In-Port has been developed. This is generally used for small peripherals such as a mouse and can save valuable serial ports for other peripherals.

The Power Supply

Only mentioned for completeness but very important. The mains power supply is converted here into low voltage DC supplies for the electronics of the computer.

Expansion Slots

An important part of any PC, these allow additional boards - such as modems, memory expansion, network cards etc. to be fitted to the machine.

Peripherals

The standard PC has one input device - the keyboard and one output device - the display unit or "monitor".

As we will see, a PC is a wonderful machine for performing all kinds of work. It is however very limited in its applications without "peripherals". These are devices which connect to the machine's own expansion ports or slots. They allow the PC to receive different types of input and produce different types of output.

Input Devices

The Mouse

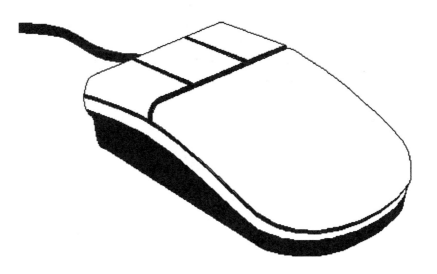

Used for easily moving a cursor around, mainly in a
graphical environment (described later).

The Graphics tablet

An alternate way of moving the cursor, often used for
Computer Aided Design (CAD) workstations.

Scanners

A means of "digitising" images to allow them to be
stored and edited on the computer and included in other
documents.

The Joystick

A joystick is often used as an alternative way of moving a cursor or other object around the screen. As its name suggests, it is like a miniature aircraft joystick and gives added realism to many games - flight simulators in particular. To be able to use a joystick with any program, there must be a suitable "games" port in which to plug the joystick's connector. The software itself must also be supplied with the necessary "driver" so that it recognises the signals from the joystick.

Output Devices

Plotters

Often used for high-resolution and large-scale output on CAD systems.

Printers

The most widely used peripheral, used for producing a "hard copy".

There are several different types of printer, all using different techniques and providing various levels of print quality:

- Dot-Matrix

- Bubble Jet

- Laser

- Thermal

For serious work requiring good print quality, a laser printer is preferred.

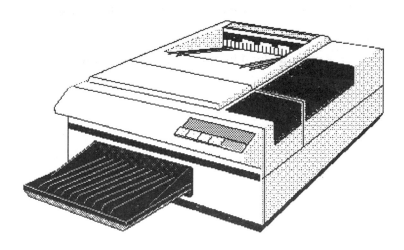

A typical laser printer

Combined Inputs and Output devices

Modems

The word "modem" is derived from the terms MOdulator and DEModulator and this may give a (very) small clue as to its intended function.

A modem is used to connect a computer's serial port to a telephone line, to enable it to transfer data via the telephone network to a remote computer anywhere in the world.

Fax modems

Similar to a data modem, a fax modem is used for the
direct transmission and reception of faxes, without
having to first print out the document to be faxed.

There are other types of peripherals but this will now have
given you a basic understanding of the ones you are most likely
to encounter.

Chapter 6. Programs and Data

Now LET US turn our attention to a less tangible subject - the software.

Software is the name given to the programs and the data which reside on the computer. Software "files" cannot be seen - they are not physical devices - but are nevertheless vital to the computer.

Files

A File is the name for a single item of software as stored on the computer. There are just two main types of software files. A file can either be an "executable file" - a computer program such as a word processor - or a "data file" - a group of data items for use with a computer program, such as the contents of a letter or other documents.

File names

We must give any file a name so we (and the computer) can recognise it. The file name must conform to certain DOS conventions, as follows:

FILENAME.EXT

This file has the name **FILENAME** and the extension **EXT**.

Generally, the name is used to *describe* the file, and the extension is used to indicate the *type* of file.

The name can contain up to eight characters[7]. These can be any alpha or numeric character plus many of the punctuation characters. Some characters are not allowed, such as \, * and ? which all have special meaning to DOS.

Each user may have their own preferred way of naming files but it is good practice to adopt a consistent set of standards within any one company.

Example file names

word.exe	Word Processor program
menu.bat	Batch file for displaying a menu
letter_1.doc	My first letter!
sales_93.dat	Sales results for the year

Used correctly, file names can make a computer system far easier to understand to the operator and to anyone else using the same machine.

Programs / Applications files

A program or application file can be thought of as a collection of commands which enable the computer to perform a particular task. This might be the complete instructions for a complex database program, or maybe a simple program to add together two numbers. (These files are called "executable"

---

[7] *This assumes that we are using the MS-DOS operating system, described in chapter 7. This will be the case on the vast majority of PCs. DOS does not differentiate between upper case (capital) and lower case (small) letters for file names or commands, although some operating systems do.*

files). It might even be simply a series of DOS instructions (commands) which instruct the computer to perform a particular sequence of actions. This particular type of program file is called a batch file and is something that can easily be created and used even by a relatively novice user. We will examine batch files in more detail later.

In order for a program file to be recognised as such by the computer, it must have one of the following extensions:

.com   command file
.exe   executable file

These are different types of program files, dependent upon their size and how they have been produced (or *compiled*). To the user, they behave identically and are both often described as "executables". For now, just think of a **.com** file as a smaller program file and a **.exe** program as a similar but larger file.

.bat   batch file

A batch file is a file containing a sequence of *DOS* and *batch* commands. This is described in more detail later in this chapter.

Data files

These files are simply a collection of related data, such as the contents of a letter (produced on a wordprocessor), the names and addresses of customers (for a database) or the sales figures for each division of a company for each month of the year (from a spreadsheet).

A data file can be given any extension (except **.com, .bat** and **.exe**) provided that it has no more than three characters and that each character is allowed by DOS.

It is usual for filenames to have semi-descriptive extensions:

wordprocessor	**.doc**
	.txt
database	**.dat**
etc.	

Often, the application will add its own (default) extension to a filename unless you specify a different one. It is generally best to stick to the default.

Special files

Within the world of DOS, there are one or two types of file worth a special mention.

Batch files

We have already looked briefly at the batch file. Such files contain lists of DOS commands which are executed in sequence until complete, when control is returned to the user (as indicated by the return of the DOS prompt). They may also contain other *Batch* commands which can be used to execute program loops and to make decisions and jump to other parts of the program. Essentially, these Batch commands form a mini-programming language of their own and allow the user to write simple (or complex) batch files.

Batch files may be used for a variety of purposes, from changing to an appropriate directory and then starting application programs, through to performing selective backup procedures.

One particular batch file is a file called

AUTOEXEC.BAT

If this file is present in the root directory of the boot drive (the disk drive that the computer loads the operating system from), this batch file will be run automatically every time the machine is switched on. This is particularly useful for performing regular tasks automatically, such as setting up the DOS **PATH** and **PROMPT** (see Chapter 11), and perhaps displaying a menu page.

Configuration files

These files affect the way the computer operates and should only be adjusted (or edited) by a computer "expert". For further information, please refer to Chapter 11.

CONFIG.SYS

is the main configuration file for a DOS system.

Utilities

These are small application programs but are usually intended to extend the functions and commands of DOS rather than to perform business or other types of applications.

Examples of such programs are disk-diagnosis, system health-check routines and "pop-up" calculators.

File attributes

A file is not just a file! It also has a number of "attributes" which can be set and reset by application programs and by the user. These should not normally affect files created and edited using standard applications packages. File attributes can be utilised by the experienced user to perform more complex batch-processing tasks.

For example, when any file is edited (i.e. modified in any way), its "archive" attribute is set. It is then possible to create a batch file which examines all archive bits. Any file which has its archive bit set can perhaps then be copied onto a floppy disk. At the same time, the batch file can be designed to reset these archive bits. Such a technique can be used to enable back-ups to be made only of files which have changed. The archive bit is represented by the letter "A".

Similarly, the read-only archive bit (R) can be used to prevent files being modified or deleted.

Two other attributes - system (S) and hidden (H) are used mainly by DOS.

Directories and Sub-directories

A Directory is simply a storage space on disk which is used to store related files. Directories have a hierarchical structure, hence a directory within a directory is called a sub-directory. A directory "tree" can therefore be created, with each major "branch" having a particular purpose. Each sub-branch then provides storage locations for similar but distinct types of work. You will find that it is far more beneficial to use a number of directories and sub-directories when organising your work on a PC, rather than lumping all files together in the root directory. Doing the latter is a recipe for long-term disaster!

In chapter 8, we will look at directories and sub-directories in more detail. Then we will examine how to create a logical directory structure in order to be able to work more efficiently.

Operating Systems

One very important and often misunderstood type of software is the operating system.

An operating system is a collection of software files which provides the basic intelligence for the computer. As we have seen, at the heart of the PC is a microprocessor - the CPU - which may be very powerful but which is useless without some means of communicating intelligently with other programs and with the user. It is the operating system that provides this intelligence.

When a computer is switched on, the operating system is automatically loaded into the computer's memory[8].

In the world of PCs, the overwhelmingly most popular operating system is MS-DOS from Microsoft - or a virtually identical version of this from IBM, called PC-DOS. All these

---

[8] *The word "booting" is used to describe the loading of the operating system. This rather strange term comes from the phrase "bootstrap loader" - pulling itself up by its bootstraps. This simply means that the CPU needs to build its own operating "environment" by loading various programs into memory. Without such programs, the machine is useless. With them, there is some means of instructing the computer to perform useful work.*

names tend to be used interchangeably, with DOS being the favourite.

Most computer "Gurus" tend to regard MS-DOS as being very primitive. For example, it can only access a limited amount of memory (640k of RAM) and can only support a single user to perform one task at any one time. That aside, MS-DOS is by far the most popular operating system of all time, with over 40 million copies sold around the world and, for most people, it provides all the facilities necessary to be able to make effective use of the computer.

It is therefore important to understand a little about what MS-DOS provides and we will cover this important topic in the next chapter.

Applications Software

Finally, we come to possibly the most important category of software. An application is the software (and user manuals) which enables the computer to perform a particular task. This might be as a database, word processor or any other function available. There are literally hundreds of different types of these application packages on the market. This topic is covered in more detail in chapter 12.

Chapter 7. A few words about DOS

As WE HAVE seen, DOS stands for Disk Operating System. This is the standard operating system used on virtually all PCs today[9]. No doubt, the term "operating system" will not yet mean a great deal to you! DOS is nothing more than a computer program that acts on commands given to it by you, the user.

DOS commands

So, what exactly is a DOS command? It is simply a series of letters which are typed by the user, immediately after the DOS prompt. Most of the commands are very descriptive of the function they perform. Here are a few commands which you may find useful:

copy file1.ext file2.ext	copies 1 file to another
dir	lists all files in the current directory
dir /p	as above, but pauses after one screen-full, prompting the user to "strike any key" to view the next screen-full
cd fred	changes to the "fred" sub-directory

---

[9] *MS-DOS actually stands for MicroSoft Disk Operating System. As we stated earlier, for most purposes, MS-DOS, DOS (and PC-DOS) are used interchangeably in the PC world.*

format a: formats a floppy disk in the
                                         A: drive

cls   clears the screen

Remember that all commands must be followed or "terminated"
by the <cr> key (often labelled with "Enter" or an arrow).

You will notice that some commands consist of only the
command letters themselves (such as **dir** and **cls**) whilst others
expect other characters to follow (**copy file1.ext file2.ext**).
These extra parts to the command are known as "arguments".

DOS commands can be internal commands or external
commands. Internal commands are recognised by DOS's own
command interpreter. This is an executable file called
command.com, which you will find in the root directory of
virtually all PCs. This file examines what has been typed in
response to the DOS prompt and if it recognises the command,
it will take the appropriate action.

      copy and **dir** are internal commands.

DOS also has many external commands. These are simply a
range of "utility" files supplied with DOS which extend the
facilities available to the user. **xcopy** and **format** are examples
of external commands. If you look at the files in the DOS sub-
directory (you will learn about utility files and sub-directories
soon) by typing at the C> prompt:

    dir<cr>

You will see a whole range of separate files whose names are
identical to external DOS commands as listed in the DOS
manual. These files are run when you type the appropriate
command.

Having said all this, there is no real difference to the user whether you are using internal or external commands, so do not worry too much at this stage if this last section was a little difficult to grasp. Once you become more familiar with the concept of running application files, it will become a little more clear.

Versions of DOS

As with all software programs, DOS is continuously being expanded and improved. The cynic might also argue that this is the way most software companies continue to extract money from the poor unsuspecting first-time customer!

There have been many versions of DOS released over the years. Version 2.1 was one of the first that became a standard for any length of time. Version 3.3 was probably the longest-lasting standard so far. Versions 4.00 (quickly followed by 4.01) was the first to break the DOS partition-size limit of 32MB for hard disks, but was not adopted widely due to suspected compatibility problems.

At the time of writing this book the current version of DOS is 6.0 (available from April 93) and already in the same year version 6.2 has been announced and it should be available within a couple of months. All these new versions coming out at ever increasing rate will not affect or change the basics covered in this book, which apply to all versions, including any future ones (as they'll have to be upward-compatible)!

You can easily establish which version your own PC has by typing

```
ver<cr>
```

Wildcards

DOS expects precise commands but it is possible to include "wildcards" within commands as follows:

> *   means any valid combination of characters.
>
> ?   means any valid single character.

The command **dir letter?.*** will list all files with filename:

> `lettera`
>
> `letterb`
>
> `letter1`
>
> `letter2`
>
> etc

and with an extension of any valid combination of 1, 2 or 3 characters.

For an exercise, see if you can work out which files the command

> `dir a?a*.da?`

would list.

Other operating systems

There are many other operating systems in use on computers in the world, but not many are in regular use on personal computers.

You may hear of:

OS/2	IBM's own challenge to Microsoft's MS-DOS and Windows
UNIX	Used more on larger mini-computer systems but with some specialised applications on larger PC installations
XENIX	Pronounced ZEENIX, substantially the same as UNIX
PICK	Ideal for databases, again mainly on larger systems

Some of these operating systems offer advanced facilities such as multi-tasking and multi-user operation and others are designed for specialised applications.

However, for most everyday uses, DOS is likely to be the preferred operating system for many years, simply because of the enormous range of applications and support in the world today.

Chapter 8. Using your Computer

HAVING STUDIED SOME of the theory, now let's get down to the interesting bit! For this section, it will be very helpful if you have the use of a PC to actually work through the sample exercises. If not, do not despair. You will still find many useful tips which will help you to use computers in future.

Creating your workspace

When working on a computer, your program files and data files can be stored anywhere you may choose on the disk - all in the same directory if you wish, providing there are not two files of the same name.

This is not good practice however, as the computer's disk would soon become full of hundreds and hundreds of programs. These would be impossible to manage easily and soon, it would become a nightmare to unravel the different applications and data files.

To avoid this situation, it is usual to have different sub-directories for each application program, for each user, and maybe yet more sub-directories for utilities and tools. These can be thought of as separate compartments or "filing drawers" of the disk drive. The exact structure of these sub-directories is entirely at the discretion of the person in charge of the PC. Different people have their own ways of structuring their system. What is important is that this structure should be understandable, logical and easy to manage.

If you are using a computer that is "owned" by someone else, you will have less control over the directory structure used, but you should still create your own workspace to ensure your own files do not become mixed up with those of other users. After all, you cannot control the names of files created by other users. Using your own workspace (i.e. your own sub-directory or directories) will avoid any possible confusion here. So, before using a computer always create your own working directory or directories.

A simple directory structure

The following directory tree provides a good basis for structuring the hard disk on a simple system used by more than one person. This will suit many small-business applications. In some cases, you may also find that you need an area of the directory tree where more than one person can operate, such as for project files or for files which are needed by more than one person. In this case, it may be appropriate to create sub-directories for projects or for accounts, letters or sales contacts. As I said before, it depends on the exact use - and on personal preference.

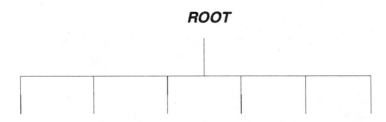

ROOT

DOS   WORD   SPRDSHT   DBASE   FREDA   BILL

A more advanced directory tree

The following diagram shows a more complex directory structure and this demonstrates how the previous directory tree can be expanded to meet the growing requirements of the users.

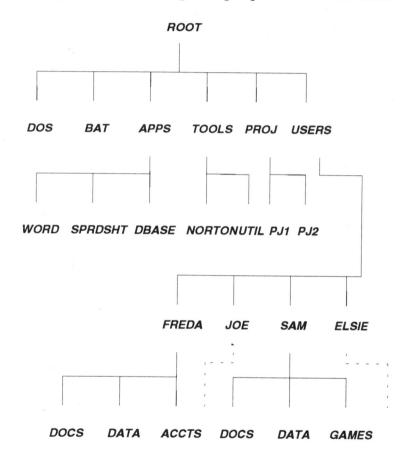

Here, four users each have their own directory space, created under a common "USERS" directory, and three main application files also have their own sub-directories under a common "APPS" directory.

Techniques such as this make the system far easier to understand and manage.

Now, here are a few exercises for you to try out on your own PC to further illustrate the concept of sub-directories and files:

Exercise - To create your own sub-directory

Objective:

To begin to use DOS by creating your own workspace

We will now assume that you have the use of a PC and that it is switched on and displaying the **C:\>** prompt.

When attempting all exercises, do not forget that all DOS commands must be terminated (followed) by pressing the ENTER or <cr> key on the keyboard. Type the commands exactly as they appear in the text, using spaces where, and only where, spaces are shown. (DOS is not bothered whether you use capital or small letters for any command, but I suggest that you stick to small letters for now. This will make it easier to compare your entry with that in the book, in case of difficulty).

First, we will look at all the files in the root directory of the computer. Type the following command:

```
dir
```

You will probably see a large number of files displayed. Typically, there will be more than one screen-full. To enable us to examine these files more easily, type the following command:

dir /p

If you previously had more than one screen-full of file names, you will now see that the display stops scrolling when the screen is filled and that a prompt is displayed inviting you to

press any key to continue . . .

You may type (nearly) any key here, but it is usual to use the spacebar (the long bar at the bottom of the keyboard) or the <cr> key. Press one of these keys until the DOS prompt returns to the screen. (If you have less than one screen-full of file names in the root directory, this second command should have had no different effect compared to the first command entered).

You have now given your first instruction to your computer!

Let us now experiment with some further DOS commands in order to become more familiar with "talking to" your computer.

First of all, make your own sub-directory. For this we use the DOS command **md**. (This is actually a shortened form of the instruction **mkdir** and you can type this instead of **md** if you wish. Most PC users tend to use **md** though).

md   myname

(Note that you can choose any valid combination of eight characters for "myname").

Now, change to that sub-directory using the DOS command **cd**.
(Again, this is short for the fuller command **chdir**. The two can
be used interchangeably).

> `cd myname`

Now, have a look at files in your sub-directory using the **dir**
command.

> `dir (you won't need "/p")`

There are no files of course as this is a new sub-directory. Just
to confuse things a little, you will see that DOS reports the
presence of two files! What can these be? The files are actually
called ".". and "..". They are used by DOS to identify where this
particular sub-directory belongs in the overall directory tree
structure. We will discuss these apparently non-existent files in
a moment. For now though, let us continue with the exercise.

We will now copy a file from the root directory into our new
sub-directory, in order that we have a file to work with. Type
the following command:

> `copy \autoexec.bat test.bat`

The "\" tells DOS that the file we are copying is in the root
directory. Note that we have not put a "\" character before the
name "test.bat" otherwise this would have told DOS that the
new file should also be placed in the root directory.

Now, copy another file from the root directory

> `copy \config.sys test.sys`

and now look at the files in your sub-directory

> `dir`

You will note from this that copied files do not need to have the same file name as the original.

I have of course assumed that your computer has these two files in the root directory, which is why I have chosen these particular file names. They are simply two text files which DOS reads at start-up (when the machine is "booted" or switched on) and should be present on virtually every PC. If for any reason your computer does not have these files, you may of course use the **dir** command to identify files in the root directory and substitute their names in the above example.

Now, delete one of the files, using the **del** command:

```
del test.bat
```

Look at files in your sub-directory, and you will see that there are now only three files reported (one real file).

```
dir
```

Now, delete all files in your sub-directory, using the "*" wildcard.

```
del *.*
```

Notice that you are prompted to confirm such a drastic action!

Type the confirmation

```
y
```

and again, look at your sub-directory

```
dir
```

All the files have been deleted, except the two special directory files.

Go back to the ROOT directory by typing the command

```
cd \
```

and remove your sub-directory, using the **rd** command

```
rd myname
```

As with the other "directory" commands, this is again an abbreviated form of the command **rmdir**.

If you try to remove a directory with this command when it is not empty, DOS will not allow you to do this. This is a very necessary protection as otherwise, the deletion of one sub-directory may result in the loss of many files and sub-directories.

This completes our first exercise with the PC and you now know how to:

- Create a sub-directory
- Change the working directory
- Copy files from one place to another
- List all files
- Delete files
- Remove a sub-directory

Returning now to the subject of our two mysterious files, "." and "..", these files are essential to DOS in keeping track of the directory structure that is created. To demonstrate this, you may wish to try creating a further level of sub-directory under your own directory and then changing to this directory (using the **cd** command). Type

```
dir
```

and you will again have two more files with the same names, ".".
and "..". If you now type

```
cd ..
```

you will move back to your original sub-directory. This
demonstrates that ".." is the address of the "parent" directory to
whichever sub-directory you are currently working in. This
applies wherever you are in the directory structure (other than
the root directory, of course).

Having now experimented with these first few DOS commands,
the following exercises will give you a little more practice and
should help to further de-mystify the inner workings of the PC.

Exercise - Create your own workspace and copy some files

Objective:

*to become more familiar with directories and with several DOS
commands*

Create a working directory	**md mydir**
Change to it	**cd mydir**
Copy a file	**copy \autoexec.bat**
Copy it to another file	**copy autoexec.bat fred.doc**
Look at the directory	**dir**
Copy another file	**copy \command.com test.com**
Take a backup copy	**copy test.com test.bak**
Look at the directory	**dir**

We will now introduce a couple of new DOS commands:

Examine the file   **type autoexec.bat**
Examine the copy   **type fred.doc**

The "type" command causes the contents of the file to be displayed on the computer screen.

Rename the copied file   **ren fred.doc test.doc**

The DOS command "ren" simply replaces the filename with a new one. For this command to be carried out, the file must exist under its original name, and the new name must be a valid DOS name.

Look at the directory again   **dir**
Recreate Fred   **copy test.doc fred.doc**
Look at the directory again   **dir**
Delete Fred and Test   **del *.doc**

The wildcard "*" is used to specify any file with the extension "doc".

Look at what is left   **dir**
Now delete these files   **del *.b??**

Here, we are using a combination of wildcard characters to specify any file with a 3-letter extension which begins with the character "b".

Look at what is left   **dir**
Now delete everything   **del *.***
(Answer with a "Y")

Check nothing is left   **dir**
Back out of your directory   **cd ..**
Finally, remove directory   **rd mydir**

(End of Exercise)

By now, you will hopefully be beginning to feel a little more confident about typing on the PC keyboard and will be beginning to understand the concept of sub-directories and files.

You should also now have an insight into a few more basic DOS commands.

Here is one more exercise which introduces further commands:

Exercise - Identify which applications are present on the PC

(Again, don't forget to type <cr> after each command line)

Ensure you are in the root directory   **cd **
Display the directory structure   **tree**

The "tree" command produces a graphical display of the directory structure on the computer screen.

Any program files?   **dir *.com**
                              dir *.exe

Find directories   **dir *.**

Use the "dir" command to find files without any extension. This can be a simple way of listing directories, although beware that it is possible (but unusual) to have a directory name which itself has an extension).

Change to a likely sub-directory. e.g.   **cd dir1**

Use the directory name to judge whether there may be any program files in the directory (a directory called "data" is unlikely to contain any executables!).

Are there any executable files?   **dir *.com**
                                    dir *.exe

Now, you have to repeat this for every other sub-directory!

To do this, you will need the following commands as well:

Return to the parent directory   **cd ..**
Return to the root directory   **cd **

This last exercise is something you may wish to do if you start work on a badly organised PC. You must first find out about the directory structure of the machine and then painstakingly check all the sub-directories for any likely application programs. Hopefully, someone will have documented this and created sensibly-named sub-directories and batch files (maybe, even a menu system) but if not, this is the only way that you can do this using DOS.

This is therefore a good point to introduce the concept of "utility" programs. These are (usually small) application programs which provide functions which are not available in DOS and which can help enormously in using a PC.

For example, by using a utility package, such as "Norton Utilities":

One file contained within this package of utilities is designed to find any files with a particular name. This particular utility program is called "Filefind".

From root directory, type   **ff *.com**

(This assumes that the sub-directory containing the "Norton Utilities" package is specified in the "PATH" statement.)

A list of all files with an extension **.com** is displayed on the screen

Now, type   **ff *.exe**

Similarly, a list of all files with an extension **.exe** is displayed on the screen.

I'm sure you will agree that this is a little easier!

I have used this example simply to illustrate the concept of utility programs which can enhance the performance or ease of use of your computer. There are many other utilities available in the market place, including (free) public domain programs and (low-cost, try before you buy) shareware programs. Again, a glance at one of the many PC magazines will soon point you in the right direction here.

Chapter 9. "Launching" an Application

WE HAVE NOW had a good look around the PC and identified a few programs which look as though they are some sort of applications, but how do we actually start (or launch) an application program?

To do this, the computer has to be told to run the particular file in question. This can be done directly as follows:

Let us assume we have a directory called wordproc where we have installed a word processor. We will also assume that the word processor has a main program file (executable) called

wordproc.exe

In order to run the word processor application, we simply need to perform the following:

Change to the correct directory   **cd \wordproc**

Run the file by typing name   **wordproc**

You will notice that we did not need to type the file extension after the file name. DOS automatically knows to search for all types of program files under these circumstances. DOS will search for file extensions in the following order:

> **.com**
> **.exe**
> **.bat**

In the event of there being different files with the same name but a different extension, the file with the first extension on the above list will be the one that is run. To run the other files, you will have to either:

- type the filename and extension

- rename one or more files

- move similarly named files to different sub-directories

It is bad practice to have several program files with the same name and different extensions in the same sub-directory.

Running an application program from a batch file

More usually, a program will be started indirectly by running an appropriate batch file which then performs the hard work. E.g.

Run a batch file called
word.bat   **word**

word.bat then contains the following instructions:

cd \wordproc	change directory
wordproc	run the word processor
**cd **	return to the root directory

Note: When the user exits the word processor, the batch file returns the user to the root directory, before returning to the DOS prompt. It is then ready for the next command.

Creating, editing and saving your own work

When using any application program, you will often create new files. You will therefore have to decide how to name them and where to store them. Ensure you use a sensible name for any such files you may create. These files should then be stored in your own sub-directory or on your personal floppy disk.

Returning to DOS

Most application programs have a means of returning the user to the DOS prompt, ready for running another program. How this is done depends on the particular application. Often, it includes the use of the <esc> key.

DOS shells

DOS shells provide a method of quickly going into the DOS environment without "loosing your place" in an application program. Most high-quality programs have this facility, allowing a temporary switch to DOS whilst (say) in the middle of a complex spreadsheet. This instructs the computer to load a new copy of the command interpreter (**COMMAND.COM**) into the memory, but to do this without removing the existing memory contents. It is then possible to type normal DOS commands to (say) create a new sub-directory or may-be check the name of an existing file before creating a new one.

Typing

exit<cr>

at the DOS prompt allows an instant return to the application that was being run, at exactly the same place as when the new shell was loaded, without having to re-load the program and the data file all over again.

DOSSHELL

Just to complicate matters, DOS is now supplied with an alternative to the normal shell program **COMMAND.COM.** This is called **DOSSHELL.EXE** and is a sort of graphical interface, displaying information about the files, directories and system and providing an alternative way of viewing and operating your PC. If you have DOS version 4.00 or higher, DOSSHELL will be supplied.

DOSSHELL and DOS shells are two totally different concepts and should not be confused. To summarise, DOSSHELL is a particular user interface to give the user a "friendlier" way of working with DOS. A DOS shell is a means of temporarily returning to DOS from within an application program.

Running an application in Microsoft Windows

When using a graphical interface such as Windows, a different principle is used to run an application package, as compared to DOS.

As we have seen, from the DOS prompt, to run a program it is necessary to type in the filename of that program, assuming the program is either in the current directory, or in one specified in the DOS "Path".

Things are a little simpler when using a GUI. By moving the mouse pointer over the top of the required program icon - the picture which represents the application required - the (left hand) mouse button is "double clicked" (clicked twice in quick succession). Alternatively, the mouse button can be pressed just once to select the icon and the "Enter" key can be pressed to start the application[10]. A new window will then be opened on the screen, running the appropriate software.

---

[10] *You should experiment to find the more comfortable way of working for yourself.*

Chapter 10.   What might I break?

IT IS HARD to think of any way anyone could physically break any hardware by typing the wrong command into a PC. There are however a number of ways in which software files may become damaged. This chapter examines the potential dangers and suggests ways in which these risks can be minimised.

Data security

When running an application, it is the *data file* which is most at-risk. All data files contain information which is (hopefully) of some value. It is possible to delete data and even accidentally wipe the entire file -but:

> *Changes to data files are performed on temporary copies of files stored in the computer's memory. The original file is only over-written when the new work is saved to disk. If you think you have corrupted any data, exit the program without saving the changes, and start again.*

If you are editing your own file - for example, modifying a previously typed letter - it is unlikely you will do any damage to any other software. Only you know the value of your own data file.

When not to switch off

Ideally, you should exit any application and return to the DOS prompt before switching the machine off. This gives DOS the chance to close any open files and perform any other housekeeping that might be required.

Some users switch off anywhere - even in the middle of an application, and this may not cause problems since DOS will automatically close any open files the next time the machine is switched on. However, it is not wise to do this.

There are however some applications which create temporary files on the hard disk. These files are normally deleted when leaving the application. As a result, if the machine is switched off without closing the application, the temporary file will be left on the disk, occupying valuable disk space. After a while, the hard disk may become so full of temporary files that the PC can no-longer be used. Such files can usually be spotted easily. They often have filenames with an extension of

.tmp

Such files can usually be deleted without causing problems.

If the power fails

You may have lost all your work since you last saved everything to disk!

Some applications can be set to automatically back-up every few minutes. Others create temporary files. Before despairing, if at all possible, ask for help. It may save you from starting over again.

Play safe and back-up your work to disk every 30 minutes or so.

"Re-booting"

Occasionally, the PC may lock-up for no apparent reason and will no-longer respond to the keyboard. If it does, you may have just lost all your work since you last saved it to disk!

The only answer is to "re-boot" the PC, either by switching off for a few seconds, then switching on, or preferably by pressing the following keys together:

<ctrl>, <alt>, <del> (the one on the numeric pad)

Back-ups

As we have seen, you need to back-up your work to disk as you continue to create your masterpiece, but what happens if the computer's own hard disk fails? (Shock, Horror!). Yes, it can happen, and for piece of mind, data should be backed-up (i.e. copied) onto another medium, such as a floppy disk or tape drive.

Keep an up-to-date copy of all your work at all times!

Backing-up data is a very simple principle. In practice, this can become a bigger task than it might seem. You may have lots of data, it may be in different sub-directories, you may have several files with the same name......

Back-ups may be performed by copying to different media, such as to floppy disks (normal method), to a tape streamer (a bit like a cassette tape recorder, if fitted) or to a network file-server (if you are connected to such a network).

There are many different types of back-up procedure that can be adopted. It is usually the responsibility of the user to decide which is most suitable. Here is a short description of some of the options available:

Full Back-ups

All data and program files are copied each time. This can be a lengthy process which will need a number of floppy disks, depending upon the amount of information on the hard disk. A full 40MB disk might require more than 30 floppy disks!

Data Back-ups

All data files are copied each time. This takes less time and space than a full back-up and still protects the all-important files created by the user.

Incremental Back-ups

Only files which have changed since the last back-up are copied. This is by far the quickest type of back-up and can be achieved by the back-up routine examining the "archive" attribute bit of each file, as described in Chapter 6, in the section on file attributes.

The following example of a batch file shows how the "XCOPY" command can be used to achieve this:

@echo off   Stops displaying each subsequent command to the screen

cls   Clears the screen

echo Backing up...	Sends a message to the user saying what it is about to do
c:	Selects drive C:
cd\steveng\books	Changes to the working sub-directory
xcopy *.* a: /m	Using the XCOPY command, copies files to drive A:

Note the use of a Command-line switch - /m. This modifies the XCOPY command so that it only copies files which have their "archive" bit set. The /m switch also ensures that, as each one is copied, the archive bit is automatically reset.

Disk (or tape) rotation

When backing up to another media, it should be borne in mind that there is some chance that the back-up media may be faulty! You may have inadvertently bought a faulty box of disks or tapes. The way to overcome this causing a major problem is to ensure that when backing up, you have at least two sets of media, used alternately. This way, you stand the best chance of surviving most potential problems.

One final word - don't keep back-ups next to the computer. Ideally, they should be in a fire-proof safe. A good second bet is to keep them in another building (such as at home), with due regard for security and confidentiality.

Computer Viruses

You may have heard the term "Computer Virus" and wondered how on earth a virus can be caught by a computer.

Viruses are in fact nothing more than computer programs, written by software engineers with nothing better to do with their time. Such viruses hide themselves by attaching themselves to the end of another program. When the program is then run, the virus is copied into the computer's memory and then onto any other program run before the computer is switched off. If any of the programs are then copied to another machine - by floppy disk, modem or network - that machine also becomes infected.

Early viruses simply produced silly, damaging effects on the display, such as all the characters gradually falling into a heap at the bottom of the screen, erasing data on a particular date (Friday 13th is a favourite) or perhaps randomly displaying a picture of (say) an ambulance dashing across the screen at random.

The very first known virus appeared in 1986 and its author now makes money by selling virus-detection software. There is no justice! There are over 2500 known viruses but only 50 or so are common. These do variously annoying things from deleting data at random, to scrambling the entire contents of the hard disk. Not a very pleasant experience.

As these viruses have evolved, they have been designed to be more and more difficult to detect and eradicate. Modern stealth and polymorphic viruses are particularly difficult to deal with, escaping the attention of all but the best anti-virus software.

They are also much more insidious, perhaps gradually modifying the contents of important data files so it is difficult to detect when the problem actually started.

So, having now scared everyone, how should the everyday PC user prevent being caught out by a virus?

The answer is two-fold.

First of all, ensure that all incoming software is "virus-checked" using a reputable and up-to-date anti-virus package. Even then, it is possible (but unlikely) for a new virus to escape from being detected. Free games software can be particularly bad for this.

Secondly, only use software from recognised sources, and do not swap your disks with friends or acquaintances. They may unwittingly be giving you a hidden present!

Chapter 11.   A bit of Troubleshooting

HAVING NOW LEARNT some of the basics of a PC system, you can now confidently sit down at any PC, find your way around it, and start to use it in a productive way...... or can you?

We have explained why a computer can be classed as "PC compatible", it is only reasonable for you to assume that they will all behave in exactly the same way when they are turned on.

Of course, nothing is ever as simple as it may first seem! However, once we start looking at how a computer is configured or set up, we soon realise that two apparently identical PCs can behave very differently.

This is a complex subject. We will therefore only skim the surface of this topic here. This will give you an appreciation of ways in which computers can be set up and how these differences may affect the performance of the PC.

The "Configuration" of the Computer

Computers have a number of special files which affect the operation of the computer and allow the user to tailor the system to their own requirements. DOS automatically examines and runs these files when it is first loaded. As the files can be modified by the user, the start-up and operation of the machine can be dramatically altered, as required.

config.sys

This is a special file which tells the machine to load certain programs (such as mouse and graphics drivers).

autoexec.bat

This file is a batch file which is "run" immediately after
DOS has been loaded and determines what the
computer does when switched on. Depending upon its
contents, it may do little, leaving the user with the DOS
prompt. It may however automatically run an
application (e.g. word processor or Windows) or
perhaps display a menu for the user.

The "Prompt" command

The DOS prompt tells the user that DOS is ready to
receive a command. One of these commands is the
"PROMPT" command which is used to instruct DOS to
alter the type of prompt that it uses. This command is
often issued in the autoexec.bat file and can totally alter
the otherwise familiar DOS prompt - C:\>. This is set
using the line

PROMPT PG<cr>

Some people like to see their name on the screen all the
time. The command

PROMPT STEVE $G Ready

Would result in the DOS prompt:

STEVE C:\ Ready

If you look at the contents of your **AUTOEXEC.BAT**
file, you may find a similar line. To examine the file, try
using the DOS command "TYPE".

At the DOS prompt, type

TYPE AUTOEXEC.BAT<cr>

As always, remember that you need an Enter or <cr> to terminate the command.

The "Path" command

The PATH command tells DOS which directories it must search and in which order it must search them to try to find a program file. If no path is set, DOS will only search the current directory for that file.

path=C:\dos;C:\wordproc;C:\sprdsht;C:\util

The above line in an autoexec.bat file will subsequently cause DOS to first search the current directory, followed by all sub-directories defined in the "path" statement whenever a filename is typed.

This feature is often used for running applications which are stored in their own directories and when the current directory is set to a data directory.

Set-up

In the days of the original PC there were a number of switches on the motherboard which had to be set to match the "set-up" of the computer; how much memory, hard disk, type of display, etc. all had to be configured prior to switching on the computer.

With the advent of more and more powerful machines with ever increasing options, it became impractical to set up the machine in this way. As a result, newer machines are now built with small amounts of battery-powered memory. This memory is used to store such settings in a semi-permanent manner and only alterable by running a special "Set-up" program. (Very) occasionally, these settings may become corrupted[11] - perhaps because of a faulty battery (such batteries last from 5 to 10 years) or because of some other fault. If this happens, a message will be displayed when the machine is switched on advising the user of the problem. If this should happen to you, I would recommend that you refer the machine to someone more familiar with computers, rather than attempting to cure the fault yourself. You risk loosing valuable data.

Country Dependent Settings

Yet another factor affecting the exact way in which a PC operates is the "Country" setting defined by the person who originally configured the machine. These settings affect a number of factors, such as the format of the date display, the exact keyboard layout in use and the character set displayed on the screen. For example, some European countries use characters with accents and these are not available on US or UK keyboards and screen displays. If the characters on the screen do not match some of the less frequently used keys on the keyboard, it is likely that these setting are incorrect. Such settings are explained in detail in the MS-DOS manual but again, it may be better to call on the services of someone more familiar with PCs than risk rendering the machine temporarily unusable.

---

[11] *"Corrupted" is a term used to indicate that a software file has been inadvertently modified, perhaps due to a hardware or software fault or even due to a virus.*

DOS error messages

Once MS-DOS is in use, there are a number of error messages which may be displayed from time to time - usually as a result of commands being typed incorrectly. Here are a few of the more common ones:

Bad command or filename

DOS does not recognise what was typed either as a valid command or as a valid name of an executable file

Incorrect DOS version

The program that you are attempting to run requires a different version of MS-DOS

Not ready reading drive A
Abort, Retry, Fail?

DOS has tried to read from (or write to) a disk in drive A and has discovered that no disk is present. Insert a disk and type

R

(Retry). If you do not wish to read from drive A, typing

A

(Abort) will instruct DOS to return to its previous state. However, if you have changed the default drive to A:, DOS will continue to try to read from this drive and hence will still not be able to find a valid disk drive. The only way out is then to type

F

(Fail). This will tell DOS that you have made a mistake. However, DOS will not know which drive to use and will ask for more information by displaying the message:

Current drive is no longer valid>

To the uninitiated, it is not obvious that DOS is requesting that you enter the new default for the drive (probably C:). Typing

C:

will take you back to the DOS prompt once again.

There are many other DOS error messages, which vary from one version of DOS to another and which are listed in the DOS reference manual, for anyone with a curious inquisitive mind.

Finally, remember that MS-DOS is very unforgiving. It expects commands to be typed exactly in the format specified and will always try to do what you tell it to. This may not always be what you intend!

Re-booting

At switch-on, the PC "comes to life" by loading the operating system - usually from the hard disk. As we have already seen, the PC first looks for an operating system in the first floppy disk drive - drive A: as it is called.

There is a very good reason for this. It is possible that there may be a need to load a different operating system at start up. For example, the "System files" on the hard disk may have been corrupted or the PC may be used by other people for specialist applications.

The PC therefore attempts to load the operating system from drive A: and if it is successful, it gives the user an A: prompt. If no disk is present in the drive, it will then look to load the operating system from the hard disk (drive C:) and will give the user a C: prompt.

This is a useful facility for the computer "expert" but can be a source of problems for the new user. If there happens to be a floppy disk in the A: drive, the BIOS is clever enough to recognise that there is a disk present, but it is not clever enough to deduce that if that disk does not have the operating system files on it, it should continue and load them from the hard disk. Instead, a cryptic message appears on the screen saying:

Non-System disk or disk error
Replace and press any key when ready

All that is needed is to remove the offending floppy disk and press any key on the keyboard, but this is less than obvious to the uninitiated!

To add further confusion, if the floppy disk happens to contain operating system files - i.e., if it has been formatted with the command

FORMAT /S

(see Chapter 5), the computer will obediently load the operating system from the floppy and will not then behave as might have been expected.

A simple check before switching on, to ensure there is no floppy disk in the A: drive will prevent such problems.

Chapter 12. Popular uses for a PC

To MANY PCs may be thought of as being used as simple word processors or maybe for the occasional spreadsheet, or even simply for playing games on. In actual fact, over the past six or seven years, PCs have infiltrated almost every aspect of business life and have become essential tools for many different departments.

There are thousands of application software packages on the market, with many alternatives which perform essentially the same task. Here is a taste of typical uses that these versatile machines can now be used for.

Word Processing

Word processing is undoubtedly one of the most common applications for the office PC, enabling the production of professional quality business correspondence.

In its most basic form, a word processor allows the typing, correction and subsequent modification of a document - perhaps a letter or a report - without the typist having to re-type the whole document each time, as would be the case with a typewriter. With a word processor, text is stored in the computer's memory and is modified on the computer screen prior to printing and / or saving as a computer file.

The first word processors were actually developed to assist computer programmers with the task of writing and modifying computer programs. There are many simple "text editors" still sold for that purpose.

In addition to these basic editing facilities, modern word processors have many other powerful features, such as spelling checkers, grammar checkers and mail merge[12].

More recently, graphical word processors - running under the Windows system - have become very popular, displaying an almost exact screen display of the document, including the use of graphics (such as a company logo or a bar chart) or larger text "fonts".

This facility is known by the now famous acronym "WYSIWYG" - what you see is what you get(!) and is a very powerful tool for producing professional quality documents.

There are many different word processors in use in the PC world. Famous names include Microsoft Word and WordPerfect, both having versions running under DOS and Windows.

Spreadsheets

The second-most common PC application is the spreadsheet and it was this particular type of program - a program called VisiCalc - that so contributed to the success of the very first personal computers from Apple in 1978.

A spreadsheet is nothing more than a matrix of "cells" each of which can contain text, numbers or formulae - a sort of computerised graph paper. Each cell is referred to by its column and row "address". i.e. the top left hand cell is known as A1.

---

[12] *Mail-merge is a facility available with many word processors where a standard letter can be "merged" with a database of names and addresses to generate individually addressed and personalised letters.*

The following simple example should serve to illustrate this a little more clearly.

	A	B	C
1			
2	Jones Wheelbarrows Ltd		*Northern Area Sales*
3			
4		Unit Price (£)	20
5			
6	Month	Sales Volume	Value
7			
8	Jan	200	4000
9	Feb	210	4200
10	Mar	240	4800
11			
12	Total, Q1	650	13000

This simple example contains text - for headings, names of months etc. - together with numbers - for sales price and sales volume - plus a number of formulae. For example, Cell B12 contains the formula "=sum(B8,B10)". This tells the spreadsheet to calculate the sum of cells in the range specified, and then display the result in that cell. Cells C8, C9, C10 and C12 also contain formulae.

The spreadsheet above calculates the sales value per month and the total for the first quarter (Total Q1) based upon a selling price of £20 per item. If the sales price (in cell C4) is altered, all sales values are immediately re-calculated. Similarly, if the sales volume for any month is changed, the effects of this can be seen instantly.

Many types of functions can be included in formulae to simplify even the most complex calculations. Such functions vary a little from one spreadsheet package to another and generally include ones for a wide variety of arithmetic, statistical and logical purposes.

Spreadsheets are versatile tools, often used for instant financial analysis, with the ability to perform such "what-if" calculations to support the decision making process. At a simpler level, they can also be used for sales forecasting, budgeting, expenses and even personal bank/finance records.

Microsoft Excel, Lotus 1-2-3 and CA-SuperCalc are all examples of popular spreadsheet programs for the PC.

Many spreadsheets also support some form of graphics facilities, allowing you to pictorially represent such results. Here, we can clearly see the sales trends over the three months in question by using a bar chart.

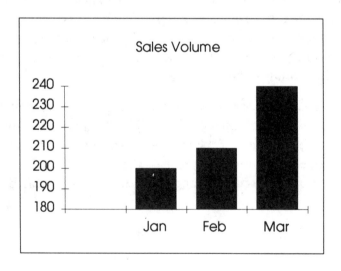

Different types of graphics can usually be produced, such as pie charts and three-dimensional bar charts. This enables the user to select the one that is most suitable for illustrating the particular type of information being displayed.

Databases

The third "classic" application of a PC is as a database. Consider the many different requirements for data within a typical business:

Details of customers and suppliers	Names and addresses Telephone / Fax numbers Sales history records
Stock records	Re-ordering requirements Stock levels Slow-moving goods
Customer support records	Records of equipment installed History of faults Statistical analysis of faults in equipment in the field
Personnel Details	Employment history Records of achievements Sickness records

There are many more categories - dependant upon the particular business concerned but these should serve to illustrate the types of applications possible.

Usually, data records are entered into a database by typing details onto "forms" on the screen. These forms are representative of a paper form that might be filled in to gather the same information, and have to be designed for the particular application in mind.

Once data is entered into the database, it is then possible for reports to be generated. This action is known as a database *"enquiry"*. Some databases may ask the user to fill in details on an enquiry form and others may operate using a "query language[13]". For example, a user may wish to make a particular enquiry on a holiday database at a Travel Agent:

> "List all package holidays available for Gran Canaria, in full-board accommodation on the second or third floors in south-facing rooms, for 2 adults and 2 children, travelling between the 4th and 18th August, departing London Gatwick between 09.00 hrs and 11.00 hrs, ..."

The thought of finding this out by wading through dozens of holiday brochures and the resultant long queues and disgruntled customers and staff at Travel agents would soon put many people off foreign holidays. Of course, the results of such an enquiry are only as accurate as the data in the database. Again, the adage "Rubbish in, rubbish out" is very appropriate!

---

[13] *A Query Language is a means of writing English-like questions or "queries" in order to interrogate a database. In this way, it is possible to enquire about virtually any detail without the need for this enquiry to be pre-programmed into the system. SQL - "Structured Query Language" is becoming an industry standard for such applications.*

Databases are one of the most natural applications for a computer network, where different people need access to the same basic data. Typical uses include the maintenance of records of customers and suppliers, and for production information, such as stock records etc.

DBase, Approach, DataEase, Microsoft Access and Paradox are all examples of popular database packages in use in the PC world.

Other applications

There are many more applications that we could cover in detail, but that is not the real purpose of this book. For the record, though, here is a brief overview of the next most popular PC applications.

Desk-Top Publishing (DTP)

With the advent of GUIs, desk-top publishing systems have become well established as a normal extension to the functions offered by word processors. The combination of graphics, text and layout capabilities means that desk-top publishing can be used for professional in-house production of marketing literature, news letters and other complex documents.

Favourite packages include Aldus Pagemaker, Ventura Publisher, Page Plus and Quark Xpress, which has been recently released for the PC, having made its name as the favourite DTP package on the Macintosh.

Graphics design

The original industry standard for PC-based graphics design was a package called PC-Paintbrush. As with most other applications, by today's standards, this original package was a little primitive and several powerful professional graphics packages are now readily available. They are extremely versatile and can be used for industrial design, logos, technical documentation illustrations, and most types of diagrams.

corelDRAW! , *Design*works and Professional Draw are examples of such packages.

Accounting packages

Many small (and not so small) businesses run their accounting systems using PCs. Such systems provide the normal facilities for double-entry bookkeeping - Sales and Nominal Ledgers, Trial Balance, Invoice generation etc. - at a relatively low cost to the business. Some also offer links into Sales Order Processing, Payroll and Stock Control systems.

Sage Financial Controller, Tas books, Pacioli 2000, and Quicken are all packages which you may encounter in this field.

CAD - Computer-Aided Design

CAD is a specialist drawing system which effectively replaces the draughtsman's drawing board. It is used for two and three dimensional (2D and 3D) technical design-drawings in mechanical engineering design, printed circuit board layouts and for complex simulation purposes. CAD is often associated with computer numerical control (CNC) lathes and other machines. This type of system is known as "CAD/CAM".

AutoCad is by far the most successful drawing package for the PC, offering advanced 2D, 3D and solid modelling facilities.

Project Management

There are a number of standard techniques that have been used for many years in the control of large projects. PERT analysis, GANNT charts, critical path analysis, time-scale calculations, cost analysis etc. are all important tools and methods in project management. High-quality low-cost PC software is readily available that automates and simplifies these techniques and allows them to be used cost-effectively for the control of a wider range of projects than with manual or mini-computer based systems.

CA-SuperProject, Project Manager Workbench and Microsoft Project are leading packages in this specialised field.

Communications

Communications programs are available for enabling computer-to-computer links for transferring files, remote control of processes and remote access to central databases. In the office, they are most commonly used - in conjunction with a modem - for transferring files from a remote desk-top or lap-top computer to a main file server or desk-top machine (or vice versa).

Some communications software also supports fax modems, allowing the sending and receiving of faxes to and from other fax machines.

ProComm, Telix, Relay Gold, Terminal (supplied with Windows) and WinFax Pro are common examples of such communications software.

Software Development

An important and very specialised application for PCs is their use as a software development "tool". In fact, the PC is arguably the best possible machine for developing PC-software applications. Any such program can be instantly tested on the machine in which it was developed.

Packages such as Microsoft C, Visual Basic and Turbo Pascal provide programming languages and development tools to enable software engineers to design and test new application software.

Education

Finally, it should not be forgotten that PCs are now well established in schools and colleges both as educational tools and for administration purposes, having now virtually replaced many of the original "home-computer" type products that were originally sold into these markets.

There are literally hundreds of specialist educational software packages now available, covering all topics in the National Curriculum and more.

For further information on this fascinating subject, please refer to my book, "Computers in Schools - What parents and teachers need to know", also published by Computer Step.

Application Software in General

As you can see, there is an enormous range of software available to enable PCs to be used for a bewildering range of jobs, with many alternatives for each particular task.

Although such packages attempt to do the same job, each has its own user interface, its own set of commands and its own particular strengths and weaknesses. In addition, each one produces files which are not compatible with ones generated by similar packages from other suppliers.

Because of this, it is wise to select and stick to a particular range of application packages, learning to use them to their full capabilities, rather than to superficially learn a number of alternatives. Even then, newer, bigger and better versions of all applications are being released all the time, to provide the user with more features - and the supplier with continuing income. Make sure you have a good reason before buying these upgrades.

Chapter 13. Graphical User-Interfaces

THE "USER-INTERFACE" IS the name for the method in which the user interacts or *interfaces* with the computer. Early computers all had a simple operating system which only allowed the user to type very specific commands into the computer. MS-DOS is an excellent example of such an operating system.

There is however an ever increasing move towards what are known as graphical user-interfaces, particularly for more advanced business use.

Apple Computer Corporation caused something of a revolution when they introduced the Lisa computer in the early 1980s. This computer had a totally different way of interfacing with the user, by using icons (small pictures), a mouse and a computer screen which represented a typical desk top. This type of interface has become known as a "Graphical User-Interface" or GUI.

In a GUI, instead of a DOS prompt, the user sees a group of icons, or small pictures, on the screen. By moving a pointer over a particular icon (using the mouse) and clicking the mouse button, a window is opened on the screen, with that particular application running in the new window. The window can be any size within the limits of the screen. It can also be possible to have several application windows open at any one time.

Since the Lisa was born, a number of GUIs have become well established. Probably the best-known of these is the Microsoft Windows package, now widely used on PCs. Others include the Apple GUI as used on the Apple Macintosh (the derivative of the original Lisa) and Acorn's RISCOS operating system as used on their Archimedes computers.

It should be mentioned that, with GUIs in general and MS-Windows (shown below) in particular, in order to run correctly in a graphical environment, application packages must all be written especially for that environment. Packages written to run from the DOS prompt will not run correctly in Windows and, conversely, Windows packages will not operate without Windows itself being present.

In addition, a GUI needs more computing power and memory to produce acceptable performance to the user. Several years ago, this was a major problem, but now, most modern computer systems will happily cope with such an interface.

Today, in many businesses, Graphical User-Interfaces are being used more and more.

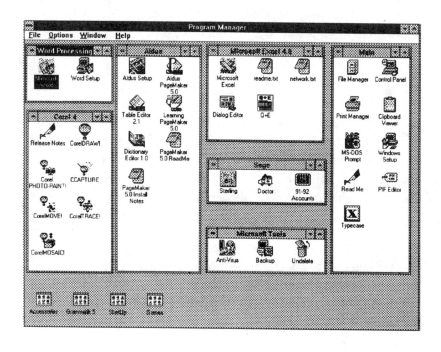

History of Graphical User-Interfaces

Although Graphical User-Interfaces - GUIs - provide a totally different approach to using computers and are now supplied with virtually all new PCs, they have not appeared overnight. The company Xerox, pioneers of the photocopier - were actually the first people to offer a GUI back in 1977 with a computer called the Xerox Star.

As we have just mentioned, the first GUIs appeared in high street computer shops in 1983, as supplied with the revolutionary Apple Lisa. For the first time, the everyday computer user was released from having to understand the underlying principles and commands of a "normal" operating system and was presented with a pictorial view of the computer and its software. In addition, a mouse was provided to move the cursor around the screen and perform tasks previously only possible by using the keyboard. This lead to the term "WIMP" interface, supposedly standing for Windows, Icons, Menus, Pointer, although many software engineers tend to use this in a more literal sense!

The Lisa was not PC compatible and was not a commercial success in its own right, but paved the way for the Apple Macintosh. The Mac, as it is known, is still not PC compatible and, for business, may be the only real desk-top alternative to the PC. However, it has a very committed following, particularly in education and desk-top publishing applications.

Microsoft Windows version 3

During this time, Microsoft were developing their own GUI, to be known as "Windows", to also compete with another PC compatible GUI called GEM from Digital Research. Neither of these products were as accomplished as the Apple but they did of course run on the PC.

Microsoft introduced Windows 1.0 in 1983. This was an attempt at such a graphical interface, but was not popular due to a lack of Windows applications and - indeed - of understanding. This was revolutionary!

Gradually, the Microsoft product began to establish itself over the less fashionable GEM and when version Windows 3.0 was launched in 1989, it was quickly accepted by virtually the whole PC industry.

Since then, version 3.1 has been released and it is now the de-facto standard User Interface for the vast majority of new PCs being sold today, with Microsoft claiming that over 1 million copies having been shipped every month since June 1992. It should however be noted that there are many more PCs out in the world that do not - and cannot - run Windows efficiently. This type of interface requires a more powerful processor, more memory, a higher resolution screen and more disk space than one simply running DOS.

Windows and the future

As we have seen there is an ever growing trend towards graphical user-interfaces, with Microsoft as the forerunner in this furious race. Let us now look at some very recent developments in Windows technology and see where that might lead to in the near future.

Windows for Workgroups is becoming the de-facto networking standard for small networks of business users, particularly where Windows itself is already in use. This provides a simple but effective Windows-compatible network without the added expense of a separate file server.

In addition, further extensions to the existing Windows multi-media facilities are being announced at regular intervals. For example, telephony interfaces are becoming available which will allow a PC to interact with an incoming caller - to enable the PC to perhaps behave as a high-performance answering machine or as a voice-mail system.

Speech recognition systems are also appearing, where commands are issued by speaking to the computer rather than by using a mouse to select items from a menu. Combining this feature with the existing speech-synthesis facilities of some multimedia systems conjures up outrageous images of PCs talking to each other - literally! Of course, in reality, they will only need to resort to this imprecise form of communications when having to deal with humans.

At the other end of the scale, Microsoft have announced a product strategy called "Microsoft at Work". In this, Microsoft see that a cut-down version of the Windows environment with the standard interface will be used for the control of hand-held machines and common office equipment - such as photocopiers and fax machines. A product called "WinPad" is to be part of this master plan for small systems and is aimed at manufacturers of hand-held products such as Personal Digital Assistants. A further variant of this adds pen-computing facilities, where - rather than a mouse - an electronic "pen" is used for entering commands. In many cases the same machine can be trained to recognise handwriting written with the same pen.

Whilst Windows is a very powerful user-interface, there are
some fundamental limitations imposed by MS-DOS which do
ultimately restrict the power of such systems. Windows NT
(new technology) is a totally new version of Windows which
overcomes this limitation. NT is a fully integrated operating
system and graphical interface - all in one. It can only run on
high-performance hardware and does not rely on MS-DOS at
all. Despite these major innovations, NT still uses the same
basic user-interface as Windows 3.1, providing a simple
upgrade path for users.

Beyond this point, however, things get a little confusing. There
are a number of very similar products being developed to do
similar jobs.

Two versions of NT already exist. One is for normal users of a
network - clients - as they are often called. This version can also
be used on fileservers. Then there is a version specifically for
file servers on high-end systems.

There will also be Windows 4.0 which is currently being
developed under the code-name "Chicago". This will be the
natural successor to version 3.1 and - like Windows NT - will
not rely on the presence of MS-DOS.

So far so good. What then confuses the issue is rumours of a
cut-down version of Windows NT, called Windows NT Lite
(Americans never could spell!). Windows NT Lite may be seen
as a direct competitor to Windows v4.0.

Only time can tell precisely how these various products will
settle into - or even create - their own niches. It certainly seems
as though one version or another of Windows will continue to
dominate the PC software scene for some time to come.

OS/2

This graphical user-interface was developed by IBM in conjunction with Microsoft and was expected (by IBM) to take over from DOS. The unexpected success of Windows 3 stopped this happening. This caused a split between IBM and Microsoft, and IBM have continued to develop OS/2 in isolation.

Recently, IBM have released a new version of OS/2, which may become more popular in the future. In many ways, it is very similar to MS-Windows.

Chapter 14. PC Networks

WHEN YOU START using a PC, you will most probably find that you will be working on a "stand alone" PC - i.e. a PC that is connected to no other computer system (it may be connected to peripherals such as a printer). You may find, however, that you are using a computer that is attached to computer network.

A network is nothing more than a number of PCs connected together, so that they can share peripherals and each other's data and programs. There are many types of networks. However, you are most likely to come across "Ethernet" and "token ring" networks. Do not worry about the differences between these, as they all perform the same basic function.

Often, there is a master PC called the "File Server" on the network. This is where most data and application programs are stored.

When using a PC on a network, the main difference that will be apparent is that you may appear to have a few disk drives which don't physically exist on your machine. These are network drives, available to all users of the network and they are part of the file server.

You can run local applications (ones installed on your PC) or network applications (on the file server) and store your data either locally or on the file server's disk.

If a company has installed a computer network, it is likely to have appointed a "System Administrator" to manage the system and to configure each machine. If so, you may well have a comprehensive menu system provided to "protect" you from the inner details of the network - such as having to know where various application programs might be located on the file server.

A well managed network will appear transparent to the user - it should not be at all obvious that you are not using a stand-alone machine.

One final word of comfort. If any problems do arise, you should have access to the network's System Administrator, who is there to help you with any difficulties you may face.

File and Record locking

For completeness, here is a quick look at aspects of computing on a network.

Due to the ability of several users having common access to files on the sever, it is usual for such files to be protected against two or more users accessing and changing data at the same time.

Simple systems use file locking. If any user has opened a file, the file is then "locked" to anyone else trying to access it. This is very effective, but can also prove to be unworkable in many situations. For example, if there are many users all wanting to access different parts of a single large database file, only one user would be allowed access at any one time. This would obviously be inefficient.

This is overcome by the more normal and more complex system known as record locking. Here, it is possible for many users to access the same file and only the individual records being accessed by each user are protected from use by any other.

Popular PC Networks

There are many different types of computer networks in use. The most popular system is called Netware, from the company Novell. Such networks are expensive, powerful and complex to set up and operate. Most companies using them will normally have appointed a System Administrator to manage the whole system.

Recently, simpler networks have become more popular with - as mentioned previously - Microsoft providing an extension to Windows called "Windows for Workgroups". This is a simple-to-use network integrated into the Windows environment and allows users to share data, printers, hard disks etc. and send messages[14] to each other. Networks can therefore also be a very useful means of improving communications in a busy office, particularly if staff are often away from their desks.

---

[14] The facility for *sending such messages from one computer to another is called "Electronic mail" or "EMAIL"*.

Chapter 15. Summary

COMPUTERS WILL CONTINUE to be more and more important to business life. Anyone who is confident in using them will therefore have an ever increasing advantage in the employment market.

Hopefully, the PC is a little less of a mystery to you now than it was before you began to read this book. You now have two choices - either to despair and forget the subject altogether or, hopefully, to "grasp the nettle" and persevere by beginning to use PCs to further build your confidence. Having gone so far, you must surely take the latter course of action. I am certain that even the most sceptical of you will soon begin to feel at home.

How to learn more

There are three major ways in which you may learn more about PCs and their applications.

First, if you look on the shelves of any medium to large bookseller or newsagent, you will find a vast array of publications devoted to PCs. Most of them contain a balanced diet of articles, suitable for the very beginner to the advanced "power-user". Titles such as PC Direct, PC Plus, Personal Computer World and PC News Weekly all contain valuable information. By reading them regularly, you will soon find yourself beginning to understand more about the subject and its jargon.

Second, as with most practical subjects, there is no substitute for hands-on experience. If you are lucky enough to have access to a PC and really do want to learn how to use one effectively, you cannot do better than sit in front of it and start typing. If you can afford to buy your own system then so much the better. PCs are now incredible value for money with quite powerful systems available for less than £600, including some software.

Finally, many colleges and other training organisations run short courses aimed at the computer novice. These can prove very effective in covering a large amount of material in a short space of time. For maximum benefit, such courses must then be followed up with practical experience in order that all this information does not disappear just as quickly.

Finally....

As you will now have gathered, the world of PCs and computing is vast - we have only just touched the tip of the iceberg - but is also one where a small amount of knowledge and experience can soon repay the investment. By reading this book, you have now taken a first and valuable step towards understanding PCs and why they are so valuable to businesses in the 1990s. With a little work, you will now find that it is a simple matter to understand enough to be able to confidently find your way around a PC and be able to run any application that is installed.

Do not be frightened of touching the keyboard. You are unlikely to damage either the hardware or the data unless you type specific DOS commands. You are unlikely to do this by accident.

Remember though, computers do what you tell them to do and maybe not what you want them to do! If the machine appears to go wrong whilst you are using it, do not panic. Instead, call someone who can give you some technical support. You will probably find they can rescue your work.

Finally, remember to backup your work regularly - to disk when using the machine, and to a separate backup disk afterwards.

I wish you every success - and pleasure - in your future dealings with these ubiquitous machines.

Happy computing!

Glossary of Terms

THE FOLLOWING GLOSSARY provides a brief explanation to many
of the less familiar terms used in this book. It also includes a
number of other industry favourites which you may come across
elsewhere. It will prove to be a valuable reference section as
you begin to delve a little deeper into this absorbing subject.

Access time
: This is the time taken for data to be retrieved
from a storage device such as a disk drive.
The lower the access time, the faster the data
can be read.

Address bus
: A group of wires in the heart of the computer
which connect together all devices (chips)
that the microprocessor (MPU) can
communicate with. The address bus is used by
the mpu to select which particular area of
memory - or section of a device - it is
communicating with at any one time.

Application
: A general name often used to describe
software packages written to perform
particular tasks of work, such as *word
processors* and *spreadsheets*, as opposed to
utilities which generally assist in the
management and maintenance of the
computer itself.

AUTOEXEC.BAT
: A batch file which is automatically run every
time DOS is re-started.

Back-ups   A means of preventing the loss of valuable work by taking copies of work done on a computer, and storing these in a different way. Usually this involves copying files to a removable disk, a tape streamer or a file server.

Batch programs   Batch programs are executable files which simply contain a list of commands to the operating system. Such files can automate common sequences of commands and hence simplify the operation of the entire system.

BIOS   An acronym for Basic Input Output System - a collection of small utility programs permanently stored in ROM and which help to match the operating system to the precise design of the hardware.

Bit   The word "bit" is short for "binary digit" and is the smallest item of data that a digital computer can recognise.

Booting   The term used to indicate that the computer is going through a start-up routine, loading the operating system files into memory. By doing this, the computer becomes progressively more "intelligent" until the operating system is fully loaded and the computer is ready to receive operating system (DOS) commands. The machine "pulls itself up by its bootstraps".

Bytes | Data processed by the mpu is handled in groups of bits, known as bytes. The number of bits handled by the mpu at one time is one measure of the power of the mpu.

CD-ROM | A means of using a compact disc to store large amounts of fixed data, rather than to store music.

Computer files | Analogous to files in a filing cabinet. Physical groups of data relating to one subject. Files can be application files (programs) or data files.

CISC | Short for *complex instruction-set computing*. Most MPUs have a range of complex instructions which simplify programming but which reduce the ultimate performance of the processor.

Corrupted files | Computers (very) occasionally fail to work correctly. This may be due to a fault in the computer, an error made by the operator, or an external problem such as the temporary loss of power. This can cause files which are in use becoming damaged or *corrupted*. The corruption may be in the form of partial loss of data or, possibly more seriously, more subtle changes to the format of the file making it unreadable by the computer. In these circumstances, back-up files can be invaluable.

CPU

The CPU is the central processing "heart" of the computer, the part which performs all the calculations and which controls all other functions of the machine.

Cursor

A flashing pointer on the screen which indicates where the "focus of attention" is. In a word processor, the cursor indicates where the next text to be typed will be inserted in a document.

Database

An application program which allows data to be stored, indexed and sorted. A common use is for storing names of business contacts and recording other information such as address, last contact date, category (such as whether customer, supplier, consultant, etc.) and any other details. Note that the use of a database for such purposes requires the user to register with the Data Protection Agency.

Data bus

Similar to the address bus, the data bus is used by the mpu to move data bytes between itself and any other hardware device connected to the bus.

Digital Format

All data can be stored in analogue or digital formats. An analogue system stores information as a continuously varying signal. A digital system converts such signals into a series of binary digits (bits). For example, an LP record stores information in an analogue manner as a constantly changing groove. A Compact Disc (CD) stores the same information digitally as a pattern of tiny holes. Hence, CDs can also be used to store other types of digital information.

Directory

As a computer file is analogous to a traditional paper file, a directory can be likened to a filing cabinet, allowing sub-directories (filing drawers) and files to be stored within it.

Disk

A rotating magnetic storage device, used for storing computer files.

Diskette

Another name for a floppy disk.

DOS

Literally, DOS stands for *disk operating system*. DOS however is also the trade name for IBM's version of MS-DOS, the industry standard operating system for the PC.

DOS error messages

DOS requires the user to type commands exactly as specified in the DOS reference manual. If commands are entered incorrectly, DOS complains by issuing terse error messages which, by themselves, can mean little to the untrained user.

DOS prompt

Simply the string of characters displayed on the screen when DOS is ready to accept a command from the user. The actual string of characters can be defined by the user and it is normal for the prompt to indicate the default drive (e.g. C:) and the particular sub-directory currently in use. Some users, however, like to alter the prompt to display the name of the company, their own name, or even the time of day!

DOS shells

A DOS shell is a temporary version of DOS loaded into memory on top of any existing applications. This allows the user to perform other task without loosing the place in the main work on the computer. A good example of this is to create a new sub-directory in order to save a newly created file. Most quality applications software allow users to "shell out to DOS", as this facility is often known.

DRAM

An acronym for Dynamic Random Access Memory, DRAM is a particular type of memory used in most computers. DRAM requires special electronic circuitry to "refresh" its memory but uses less power than other types of RAM.

EGA

Enhanced Graphics Adapter - one of the early graphics standards used in PCs.

EISA

Short for "Extended Industry-Standard Architecture", this is a high-specification bus-architecture which has been developed by a group of PC clone manufacturers. This group is headed by Compaq. The bus is an answer to IBM's MCA bus introduced on their PS/2 range of machines.

Electronic Mail Often called EMail for short, this facility allows users of computer networks to send paper-less messages to each other. Anyone logging on to a network is automatically informed if they "have mail".

Environment DOS is an operating system which can be tailored to a certain extent to the requirements of the user. The "SET" command can be used to alter a number of variables such as the PROMPT and the PATH, as required by the user. Together, these variables are known as the *environment.*

EPROM A type of read-only memory (ROM) which can be programmed and then erased, ready to be re-programmed once again.

File attributes Each file has a number of (normally unseen) attributes or markers which can be examined by the operating system and used by the user. Available attributes are READ ONLY, HIDDEN, SYSTEM, ARCHIVE. The status of these bits can be modified and displayed using the DOS "ATRIB" command.

File server The "master computer" on a network, where common applications and important data are stored.

Floppy Disk A removable storage disk which can be used for storing both program and data files.

Font

The typeface style and size, as used in a "word processed" or "desk-top published" document.

Formatting

All floppy and hard disks must be formatted before they can be used to store data. Formatting is a process which numbers the individual parts of the disk (called sectors) in order that data can be systematically stored and later retrieved.

Graphical User-Interface (GUI)

A means of displaying the user-interface of the computer by means of graphics (icons and pictures) rather than simple lines of text. Microsoft Windows has become the de-facto GUI for PCs.

Hard copy

Printed information which is computer generated is known as hard copy, as opposed to information displayed on a screen.

Hardware

Simply the name for the physical parts of a computer system.

IBM PC compatible

A machine which is PC compatible and hence will run any application software written for the PC standard.

Icons

Small descriptive pictures used with GUIs to represent applications software and hardware devices.

Input	Input to a computer can be from the keyboard, from a computer software file or from a port connected to some form of external device - such as a mouse, a modem or another computer.
ISA	ISA stands for "Industry Standard Architecture" and is the term used to describe the hardware and bus design of the original IBM PC-AT. Many clone PCs still use ISA.
Launching	A term used to describe the action of starting up an application package.
LED	A light emitting diode - often used in PCs and other electronic system as an indicator light.
Local Bus	The normal ISA bus is now very dated in design. It has major limitations for modern microprocessors such as the 486 and P5. Some manufacturers have overcome these limitations by developing a fast additional bus for connecting critical components such as memory and video cards, whilst still retaining the ISA bus for other slower devices such as disk drives and external ports.
Media	A collective term for the different types of physical devices for storing data, such as floppy disks, CD-ROM and tape streamers.
Megabyte (MB)	A measure of the amount of storage capacity (memory space) in either electronic memory (RAM or ROM) or in media. Electronic memory can be most easily expanded in

capacity by blocks. The size of these blocks (measured in bytes) is always a power of 2. For example, a Megabyte - approximately 1 million bytes - is actually 2 to the power 20 bytes = 1,048,576 bytes.

Megahertz (MHz)

A measure of the speed that the mpu operates at and one of several important factors in assessing the power of a computer. The original IBM PC worked at 4.77MHz. A fast machine today will operate at 66MHz. 1MHz equals 1 million cycles per second.

Memory cache

A small area of very fast access time RAM which is used to buffer data between the CPU and relatively slow devices such as disk drives. This can effectively reduce the average access time of the buffered device and hence speed up the computer.

Micro-Channel Architecture

Many of IBM's PS/2 machines do not conform to the original PC-AT hardware ISA standards. Instead, IBM has developed and patented a superior bus architecture, known as MCA - Micro-Channel Architecture. This allows higher performance systems to be designed than with ISA architecture but can only be used under licence from IBM.

Motherboard

The main circuit board (PCB) of the computer which contains the CPU. It is called a motherboard since it also contains edge connectors where most other PCBs in the system are plugged into.

MPU

Short for "microprocessor", this is the heart of the PC, the electronic chip which performs calculations and which reacts to commands in any computer program run on the machine.

MS-DOS

The industry standard operating system for PCs today.

Multi-media

Most PCs use a single media for storage of information - a floppy or hard disk. Multimedia systems can access more that one type of media, such as CD-ROM and Laservision Video discs. Most can also generate audio sounds. Hence, they can be used for more complex applications such as interactive video and advanced computer-based training applications. In 1990, Microsoft devised a minimum specification for multimedia systems. This is known as MPC. Any machine sold as MPC compatible must have a certain minimum specification which includes a 386SX processor, CD-ROM drive and an audio card. A second generation MPC2 specification is currently being finalised.

Multi-tasking

A facility included by some operating systems. It provides a method of rapidly switching the CPU between several different application programs in order that they all effectively operate at the same time. When operating in its "enhanced " mode, Microsoft Windows is a multi-tasking system. Applications can run independently in their own windows at the same time.

MS-DOS is a single-tasking operating system.

Multi-user
A computer system which allows different users to access the system at the same time. Larger computers - mini and mainframe systems - usually have many different terminals (VDUs) connected where operators access the same computer from. Personal computers are - as their name implies - designed to be used by one person and are hence single-user machines. A network of PCs can however be considered as a multi-user system.

Network
An interconnected group of PCs of which all can access the same data, usually stored on a master unit called a "file server".

Notebook
A small portable computer, roughly the same footprint as an A4 notebook, although usually somewhat thicker and heavier. The notebook computer is hinged down one edge and opens - like a notebook - to reveal a screen and keyboard. Many notebook computers are PC compatible.

Operating system A software package which provides the basic means of communicating with the computer in order to run applications and correctly handle files.

OS/2 Developed by IBM, an alternative graphical operating system to Microsoft Windows.

Output The results generated by an application program. This may be in the form of a file, a printed document or perhaps a stream of data.

Palm-top An extremely compact portable computer. Such a machine may be PC compatible but will have a miniature keyboard and small screen and will be used more because of its portability than its useability.

Parallel port One of the standard connections on a PC where printers and similar devices may be plugged in.

Path A list of sub-directories which are specified to DOS by using the PATH command. This enables program files to be stored in their own sub-directories. These files can be run by typing their name, even if the current directory is set to another part of the directory structure. The PATH is usually set by a command which is part of the AUTOEXEC.BAT file.

Pentium Sometimes called the P5, the latest and most powerful yet version of the Intel range of PC compatible microprocessors.

Peripherals External devices such as printers which connect to the computer and extend its capabilities.

PC

Literally, short for *personal computer* - a term which can apply to any small single-user computer. However, PC is the industry standard term for an *IBM PC-compatible* computer.

PC-DOS

A term often used to mean the operating system DOS, as supplied by IBM. To the average user, DOS, MS-DOS and PC-DOS are all the same.

PCB

Short for *printed circuit board*, this is a flat board, usually made from glass-fibre, on which electronic components are mounted by soldering them to copper interconnecting tracks on the board.

PDA

A new type of portable computer system, the PDA (personal digital assistant) is a pocket-sized machine that can be trained to recognise hand-written commands and text. A PDA is more of a portable terminal - giving access to remote information via modem and cellnet telephone links - than a computer in its own right. It can most easily be thought of as a portable electronic filofax, with the potential to access almost unlimited external data.

Pixel

The smallest part of the display screen that can be individually controlled by the computer. The more pixels, the better the resolution of the display.

Program	A software program (or programme) which can be run on the computer to perform a particular task or function.
PS/2	A range of computers designed by IBM in an attempt to define a new personal computing standard and re-capture control of this market.
QWERTY	The standard UK and US layout for keys on the keyboard, so called because these are the first six letters on the top row of alphabetic keys. In Germany, the AZERTY layout is normally used.
RAM	Literally, Random Access Memory, the main type of memory in a PC, used for temporary storage of programs and data.
Re-booting	The process of re-loading the operating system. Re-booting is the term usually used to describe re-starting the PC, either by simultaneously pressing the <Ctrl>, <Alt> and <Del> keys or by switching the machine off, then on again.
RISC	Short for *Reduced Instruction Set Computer*. By restricting the MPU's capabilities to performing very simple and therefore fast instructions, a computer based on such an mpu can operate more efficiently than one using a more normal CISC mpu.

ROM
Read Only Memory. Memory used for permanent storage, even when the power is removed.

Serial Port
A means of connecting certain peripherals to a PC.

SIMMs
Single In-line Memory Modules. These are small PCB modules containing banks of memory (RAM) chips for easy expansion of the memory capacity of most recent PC motherboards.

Software
The generic term for all computer programs and data.

Spreadsheet
A particular software application which provides a means of automatically performing complex calculations and the presenting the results in clear formats - either numeric or graphical.

Temporary files
Some applications create temporary or working files which they use during the operation of the program. They are normally deleted when the application is terminated (or exited). Such files often have strange names and the extension ".tmp". If the computer is switched off whilst still running such an application, it cannot delete these files hence such files can start to mysteriously appear in sub-directories, filling up the hard disk on the machine. They must then be deleted manually to recover this lost space.

Tower

A tower system is a vertical floor-standing cabinet used for PCs which require expansion capacity - perhaps for different disk drives, CD-ROM and other add-ons. They are particularly popular for file servers on computer networks.

Turn-key system

A term used to describe a computer system that - when purchased - has already been configured for a particular purpose. Hence it will be supplied with all necessary software and peripherals.

UNIX

A complex multi-user operating system used on engineering workstations and now becoming more popular on more general purpose systems. UNIX is not normally used on PCs, although powerful file servers may sometimes run this operating system.

Utility programs

Application software which is written to perform system maintenance tasks - backing up of files, movement of groups of files to other areas of the directory structure, checking for faults on disk drives, etc.

UPS

Uninterruptable Power Supply. Such power supplies are used when computers must not be disabled by failure of the mains supply. They contain batteries which are normally trickle-charged by the mains supply so that they are always ready to for use.

VDU

Short for "visual display unit", a VDU has a keyboard and screen, just like a PC, but has no intelligence or storage capacity. Instead, it is used as an input and output device for a separate computer system.

VGA

Video Graphics Array - the most common graphics standard for PC colour displays.

Virus

A computer program designed to be difficult to detect and to cause damage to software on the computer. Viruses can unwittingly be transferred from one machine to another by the copying and passing on of software.

Word processor

An application program which allows the creation and editing of documents. Most modern word processors provide advanced features such as spell-checkers, multiple fonts and print preview facilities.

Workstation

A term often used to mean a single-user computer (often a PC) perhaps with all necessary peripherals.

Wildcard

In DOS, the ? and * characters can be used in DOS commands as *wildcards*, to specify that any allowable character or group of characters can be substituted as a valid interpretation of the command.

WIMP interface

A rather emotive acronym for "Windows, Icons, Menus, Pointer". Most graphical interfaces - such as Microsoft Windows - are WIMP interfaces.

Windows   In the PC world, the term "Windows" usually refers to the Microsoft Windows graphical user-interface (GUI).

WYSIWYG   An acronym for "What You See Is What You Get". A rather curious way of describing a system where the image on the screen is an (almost) exact replica of what will be produced on the attached printer.

Index

Best-selling books for beginners from Computer Step

The PC Novice's Handbook - 2nd. Ed.

ISBN: 1 874029 04 0

Author: Harshad Kotecha

Price: £9.95

Understand the essentials of a personal computer (PC) without
the technical mumbo-jumbo. Written for the beginner with little
or no knowledge of the PC, this is a complete guide for
choosing, understanding and using personal computers.

In clear, simple language, *The PC Novice's Handbook*
demystifies the PC. You will learn about the basic components
of the PC and the functions they perform. Then, you will go on
to software; the types available, and the features to look for.
Next you can find out how to choose your system if you have
not already made a purchase. Once you have a PC, you will
want to learn basic commands to interact with it (namely DOS).
Also, find out how your PC can talk to other computers - the
complex world of computer communications is now simplified
for everyone.

*" Everything the beginner needs to know to get started is
between these covers"*

-Practical PC

*The 1st edition was independently recommended by the
Booksellers Association as the best-selling computer book for
beginners in the UK. The new 2nd. edition is improved and
even better value!*

Computers in Schools

ISBN: 1 874029 05 9

Author: Steve Greenwood

Price: £5.95

Computers in Schools is written for anyone - particularly parents and teachers - who want to learn about the computers that are being used in ever-growing numbers in UK schools today.

What are they? Why are they being used? Do they do any good? Can they do any harm? Who pays for them? Should we buy one for home? ....if so, which one?

The list of questions is almost endless and the jargon used can often intimidate people to an extent where some become frightened of attempting to ask even basic questions about this important subject.

Computers in Schools is written in plain English. It doesn't assume any computer knowledge - in fact, all computer terms used are carefully explained.

This is an accurate, unbiased and informative book written by a concerned and knowledgeable parent. It answers many of the questions constantly being asked by parents and teachers about all aspects of computers in education.

Windows in Easy Steps

ISBN: 1 874029 02 4

Author: Harshad Kotecha

Price: £9.95

Windows is the most popular graphical environment being used on personal computers (PCs). Many computer users have already standardised on Windows.

Windows in Easy Steps is a cost-effective training guide. It combines stunning Windows screen-shots, exactly as they appear in the product, with simple, clear instructions on how to perform specific tasks - leaving out the unnecessary verbal blurb!

Windows in Easy Steps covers the current version 3.1. It shows the reader how to perform basic Windows functions as well as the more advanced ones, like Multitasking (running several applications at the same time) and Object Linking and Embedding (a way of using the same information across several applications or documents). The reader will also learn how to customise Windows and work with files, including different ways of printing.

" a handout on our Introduction to Windows Course..... a cost effective solution to providing quality, up to date course material"

-Senior Training Manager, Nat West Bank

PageMaker 5 in Easy Steps

ISBN: 1 874029 06 7

Author: Scott Basham

Price: £14.95

Aldus PageMaker is a popular desktop publishing (DTP)
software for the PC and the Macintosh. This book is a clear,
concise graphical guide; teaching all essential PageMaker
version 5 (PM5) techniques in easy steps.

As well as the basics, areas covered include: Drawing and
manipulating shapes, importing text and graphics, cropping,
skewing, reflecting and rotating objects, story and table editors,
text effects like kerning and tracking, producing table of
contents and index pages, working with colour and printing,
new aldus additions and tips for good document design.

PageMaker 5 in Easy Steps can be used as a self-teaching
tutorial and as an easy reference guide. Packed with useful tips,
it even contains information omitted from the PM5 manuals -
making it invaluable for all PM5 users.

*" .... is quite the best book on this subject I have read. The use
of concise explanations with copious pictures is the obvious
way to learn to use DTP packages and the author uses this
technique brilliantly."*

-The IBM PC User Group

DOS and all that Jazz

ISBN: 1 874029 01 6

Author: Harshad Kotecha

Price: £8.95

DOS and all that Jazz is a complete guide for beginners and intermediate users to get to grips with using essential commands and features of DOS - the most important software on a personal computer (PC).

Step by step, this book gently takes the reader from switching on the PC and installing DOS through to advanced DOS commands and concepts for managing disks, files and directories. Written in an informal, light-hearted style, it assumes no prior knowledge of DOS, or even computing.

DOS and all that Jazz covers all versions of DOS. It is a unique guide, teaching DOS through the Shell as well as from the DOS Command Prompt.

Use ***DOS and all that Jazz*** to grasp the essentials of DOS and keep it near your PC for quick reference.

" .... explains what DOS does, how it does it, why it does it, and how you get it to do it - everything the beginner is likely to want or need to know about DOS."

-PC Plus

WordPerfect: The Joy of Six

ISBN: 1 874029 08 3

Author: Darren Ingram

Price: £11.95

Enjoy learning WordPerfect 6.0 for DOS in this friendly feature-packed guide.

All the essential features (especially the new ones) are explained in a concise, straight-forward manner. In fact, much more is covered in *WordPerfect: The Joy of Six* than in many other books twice the size. For example, areas covered include:

- Editing and working with your documents
- Checking your spelling and grammar
- Creating watermarks and labels
- Colour printing, DTP and graphics
- Creating your own newsletters
- Merging files and using macros
- Performing spreadsheet functions
- Multimedia and faxability

Whether you are a novice or an experienced wordprocessor user, this book will help you to produce more effective documents.

Answers commonly asked questions and explains new features.

Training and Consultancy

Computer Step also provides training and consultancy on all areas of personal computing. For further details please contact Computer Step.

Quantity Discounts

For quantity discounts on this book or on any of our other books, please contact:

Computer Step   Tel. 0926 817999
Unit 5c, Southfield Road   Fax. 0926 817005
Southam, Leamington Spa
Warwickshire
CV33 OJH